THE NORTH ATLANTIC ALLIANCE AND THE SOVIET UNION IN THE 1980s

By the same author

COLLECTIVE SECURITY (*with Professor O. Pick*)
WARNING AND RESPONSE

THE NORTH ATLANTIC ALLIANCE AND THE SOVIET UNION IN THE 1980s

Julian Critchley

First published 1982 by
THE MACMILLAN PRESS LTD
London and Basingstoke
Companies and representatives
throughout the world

ISBN 0 333 29469 6

Printed in Hong Kong

Contents

Acknowledgements

In the making of this book I am particularly grateful for the co-operation and advice of John Eppstein, formerly Secretary General of the Atlantic Treaty Association and editor of *World Survey*, and for the generous help of John Poole, in the Scientific Section of the House of Commons Library, in obtaining the documentation which I needed.

The author and publishers would also like to thank the Controller of Her Majesty's Stationery Office, for the extract from *Written Answers*, 31 July 1980.

Part One

Basic Issues

1   The trial of strength

The purpose of this book is to trace the probable course in the next ten years of the trial of strength, which has already lasted for more than decades, between the Soviet Union, on the one hand, and the United States and its allies, on the other. It makes no prophecy. Quite unforeseen events may undo the most confident forecasts, as did the Iranian Revolution and the eruption of Islamic fervour in 1979. But it will suggest the probable evolution of the policies and armaments of both sides, in the light of available information, and examine the consequences of the present correlation of power in the world.

Any credible speculation of the future must begin by taking account of the lessons of the past. What has the experience of the first 30 years of the strategic contest between the North Atlantic Alliance and its Communist Russian rival to teach us? It has been the Soviet side throughout which has been the pace-setter, with the domination of the world by its brand of Socialism as its constant objective, with changing tactics and with rapidly growing military strength. Yet it has been proved that, on the other side, a system of collective defence can be kept up and adapted by a group of unregimented and far from bellicose peoples for the best part of a generation, even without the stimulus of imminent attack. This is encouraging; but there are already many signs that the task of reinforcing the common defensive effort with civil morale is likely to become more difficult with the passage of time, if only because of the ever-rising cost of modern weapons — disarmament by inflation — and the persistent hankering for compromise, if not appeasement, which revulsion against nuclear arms evokes. It is, of course, the *sine qua non* of a successful strategy of defence that there should be a reliable reservoir of political will upon which the government can draw. I devote a later chapter of this book to that crucial subject. It is important to remember that the striking success of the North Atlantic Alliance, so quickly constructed in 1949 after the

Communist conquest of Czechoslovakia and the Berlin blockade, in arresting the further encroachment of Stalin's military and political power in Europe, happened before men and women now in their thirties were born. It takes a greater historical sense than most of them, and even more younger people, possess to realise the significance of the peace — which, their elders would say is thanks to NATO — that they have known all their lives. That is one reason why defence and foreign affairs occupy so small a place today in the minds of the majority, a fact which is of great advantage to those who, for political motives, want to weaken the North Atlantic Alliance.

If a growing minority has been aroused in Britain during the 1970s to the need to reinforce the defensive capacity of NATO, it is largely thanks to the influence of television, not in recalling past history, but in giving day-to-day news about actual developments in the Soviet Union, its threatening military superiority in Europe, its strategic expansion in other continents and its repressive internal regime. It is evident that if the Atlantic Alliance is to remain effective during a fourth decade, a far more serious effort is needed than has hitherto been forthcoming in the Allied countries, and in particular those of Northern Europe, whose Socialist parties are particularly susceptible to the Soviet propaganda of peaceful co-existence, to educate those who can lead and inform their fellow citizens in the strategic realities confronting the nation and its allies. No-one wants the wholesale indoctrination and inculcation of class hatred to which every citizen in Soviet Russia and its satellite states is subjected from infancy. But it cannot be said that the political leaders of the West have, since the early days of the Atlantic Alliance, given their peoples a very clear picture of the basic issues involved, which are obscured rather than enlightened by arcane references to such abstractions as 'deterrence' or *'détente'* and the wishful thinking which habitually accompanies the latter.

DISSIMILAR ANTAGONISTS

What are the basic issues? The contest between the two power groups which we are studying is not the rivalry of similar entities, like the nation-states or alliances of states between which in the course of European history there have often been wars or threats of war. It is a confrontation between one great power with a global revolutionary aim, and a geographically-restricted defensive coalition of fifteen politically independent states. The former, whose rulers wear, beneath their ideological carapace, the characteristic imperialism and messianism of Tsarist Russia, is a power with a purpose. Its official dynamism is the mandate to promote the victory of Socialism over Capitalism which the Marxist—Leninist dogma declares to be inevitable, however long it may take and by whatever means.

The United States and its allies share no single *weltanschauung*, nor, despite occasional flights of idealistic rhetoric and tributes to 'democracy', have they any clear political objective beyond the defence of the deeply-prized freedom of each of them and their essential interests. The North Atlantic Treaty, like the Treaty of Brussels, which led up to it, was in origin a purely defensive reaction to an imminent military danger, namely the westward and southward advance of what used to be called 'the Russian steamroller'. The provisions and limitations of the treaty determine what the signatories can and cannot do. Each of them, twelve at first, then fourteen, then fifteen, retains complete political independence, controls its own forces, adopts its own defence budget and depends upon the concurrence of its own legislature and electorate for authority to participate in any new development of the Alliance. It is in order to protect its own national security that Germany, Britain, France and each of the smaller Allies cluster round the nuclear power of the United States and, except for France commit most of their armed forces to joint international commands under American supreme commanders. Ever since its permanent political and military organisation (NATO) came into being in 1951 under the impulse of the Korean War, the North Atlantic Council, in which unanimity is required for any substantial decision, has indeed developed more or less institutionalised forms of co-operation in strategic, and latterly, nuclear planning, arms production and financing, communications and joint training exercises etc.; but, quite unlike its opposite number, the Warsaw Pact, whose armed forces are directly controlled and their armaments standardised by the Soviet military authorities, the Atlantic Alliance retains its original character of a coalition of separate and very different states. The practical inconveniences of this are manifest, not least in the diversity of their weapons and communications systems, to cite the most obvious evidence of intractable national pride and prejudice: the open political nature of each allows for public conflicts of opinion on foreign as well as internal affairs. But for all that, there is a strength in the collaboration of free societies for their common defence which is not to be found in the enforced uniformity of a system in which national distinctions are compressed by the Russian overlord.

Considering the vigour of the different national traditions and loyalties on the Western side, it is remarkable how well the military mechanism of NATO works and it seems well-set to face the more difficult tasks of the coming years. This mechansism, controlled by the Defence Ministers, consists of the Military Committee formed by the Chiefs of Staff of the Allied powers or their deputies, to whom are responsible the Supreme Commanders in Europe, the Atlantic and the Channel. The withdrawal of the French forces from the command structure by President de Gaulle in 1967 was undoubtedly an embarrassment, but, owing to the sensible liaison system established between the French and NATO staffs, the inconvenience has been much diminished. France, while maintaining its independent control of both nuclear and conventional forces, is a valued ally and plays its part in the North Atlantic Council to which, of course, the military are subject. Co-operation at the beginning of 1980 was on the increase, both in communications and in the field of arms manufacture, and was remarkably close between the Allied navies. The military obligations of the North Atlantic Treaty are twofold: first continuous equipment for defence, secondly joint resistence to attack. The signatories undertake (Article 3) 'separately and jointly by means of continuous self-help and mutual aid to develop their individual and collective capacity to resist armed attack'; and (Article 5) 'an armed attack against any one of them in Europe or North America shall be considered an attack against them all'. In the event of such aggression against a signatory's territory, ships or aircraft in the Atlantic area 'North of the Tropic of Cancer' — subsequently extended to the Mediterranean Sea — each ally is to decide 'in accordance with its constitutional process' the means to be taken 'including the use of armed force' to assist the victim of the attack and restore peace and security in the area, a measure of collective defence recognised by the Charter of the United Nations. This mealymouthed formula, designed to satisfy the scruples of the Senate of the United States, would be quite unreal in the event of a nuclear attack, which was not contemplated when the Treaty was drafted, or even of the kind of *blitzkrieg*, attack without warning, for which the forces of the Warsaw Pact on the Central Front of NATO are known to be geared. But, in fact, instantaneous reaction to aggression, nuclear or otherwise, has always been assumed by the military planners and commanders of the Alliance, especially the Americans, as the basis of their strategy. We shall consider later the geographical limitations of the Atlantic Treaty and how the several Allies could defend their life-lines outside the restricted Treaty area.

The Atlantic Alliance, then, is itself a purely military defence organisation, though its member governments have inevitably become involved in measures designed not only to preserve the armed truce with their potential adversary but also to diminish the occasions of conflict and 'reduce tension'. This is a political operation which we shall examine in due course but which does nothing to diminish the necessity of building-up sufficient conventional and nuclear armaments to counter the vast array of preparations for land, sea and air warfare which the Soviet Union and its allies continue to accumulate. Much of this book will therefore be devoted to weaponry.

The military leaders of NATO are fond of declaring, when considering the strategy, the arms and the men of the Warsaw Pact, that they are 'concerned only with capabilities and not with intentions'. Soldiers, as a rule, prefer not to be politicians; but it is inevitably with the intentions of the Communist Party of the Soviet Union, now visibly expanding its political influence and military power far beyond the zone of confrontation with the armed forces of the Atlantic Alliance e.g. Afghanistan, as well as furthering its Socialist cause in the internal affairs of other countries that any serious student of world affairs must be concerned. How then can NATO, limited as it is to the protection of its own members in one part of the world only, be said to provide the 'defence of the West'? What we usually mean by the West is all those people whose culture and customs derive from the European or (more historically) Christian civilisation. They include in Europe, Austria, Switzerland, Sweden, Finland, most of Ireland and at present, Spain which are not covered by the Atlantic Treaty; nor is Australia and New Zealand, nor any of the Latin American countries who are certainly part of the

European tradition. Nor are the many communities in every continent who are opposed, as are the member states of NATO, to Marxist—Leninist rule. Nor again is Japan, the economic giant of Asia, which, though having none of the European roots of the Atlantic allies, shares the essential interests of the Western world. And it must never be forgotten that the most convinced believers in those fundamental civil and spiritual rights and liberties which Westerners take for granted, are to be found precisely among the millions of Europeans, Poles, Lithuanians, Germans, Czechs, Slovaks, Hungarians and Romanians who live under the heavy hand of the very power against which the defensive provisions of the Atlantic Alliance are framed. It is difficult to give any concrete expression to the sympathy which unites all those members of the human family who share similar traditions of civilisation. President Carter's attempt to secure from the Soviet rulers respect for the human rights which they had cynically agreed at Helsinki to safeguard, resulted only in the more brutal suppression of any of their subjects who had the courage to stand up for their rights. But since no tyranny has yet been eternal, there is an unquenchable glimmer of hope so long as the standards of liberty can be upheld, even at a distance. The Atlantic Alliance is not a crusade to liberate the peoples of Eastern Europe. It has not the means to do so, nor is that its object. It is justifiable, however, to speak of it as 'the defence of the West' as I have described it; for, in a certain sense, it has become *per accidens* the trustee or agent of the values of that civilisation. For apart from China, the rival Marxist colossus in the East, it is the one concentration of power which, grouped around the United States of America, is — in the light of thirty years' experience — strong enough to deter the Soviet Union from resorting to war to impose its revolutionary empire upon the world. It is not only that the United States has an awe-inspiring armoury of thermo-nuclear weapons comparable to that of the Soviet Union. Its economic strength and technical expertise are much greater; and the American people despite its defects and occasional aberrations, has proved, by its dedication to the ideal of personal liberty, that the United States is a natural focus of resistance to collectivist oppression. It is not possible to conquer the world without conquering Europe; and so long as the old nations of Western Europe, Germany, France, Britain and Italy, in particular — soon I hope to be joined by Spain — remain united in alliance with the United States in defence of the Old World and the New, they dispose of assets far exceeding most of the Soviet Union 'three times the gross national product of the USSR and four times its population', as Henry Kissinger pointed out in September 1979 at Brussels when commenting on the past and future of NATO. 'So if one looks ahead for ten years, and if we do what is necessary, all the odds are in our favour.'

The qualification is an important one; for to 'do what is necessary' involves reaching agreement between the governments of democratic countries — coalitions in some countries — in which a great variety of political, moral and emotional forces have to be faced, some favourable, some radically opposed to increasing the nuclear armoury of the Alliance, forces to which statistics of gross national products and populations are quite irrelevant. For what the former American Secretary of State regarded as a first necessity was the updating of the whole nuclear potential of the Alliance, both in the field of strategic missiles and in the case of the intermediate and tactical nuclear weapons in the European theatre. And this proved at the end of 1979 to be as clear an example as could be found of the difficulty of securing political unanimity between the United States, three of its major European Allies, Germany, Britain and Italy, and the smaller allied countries of Northern Europe, Norway, Denmark, the Netherlands and Belgium. In several of the latter, the Low Countries in particular, intense propaganda both Christian and Socialist, had succeeded in making nuclear power anathema for some sections of the population, as indeed it did for a considerable minority of Social Democrats in Germany. France remained aloof from the debate. The compromise reached in the North Atlantic Council deploying the American Pershing 2 and cruise missiles in certain allied countries but not in others, while at the same time offering to the Soviets a plan for the mutual reduction or elimination of both, may be taken as symbolic of the divided counsels which are likely in the coming years to complicate the task of the military. We can be sure that they will be exploited to the full by Soviet propaganda within the setting of the recurring negotiations on Security and Co-operation in Europe bequeathed by the Helsinki Conference. But, while the pacifist element, the environmentalist lobbies and the political Left are bound to continue, even without Soviet stimulation, anti-nuclear demonstrations which secure publicity in the media, there is a great deal of evidence to show that a majority of the thoughtful centre in each country had become by 1980 more convinced of the necessity of a strong Atlantic Alliance than they were say, in 1970. This, I believe, is true of all age groups, not excluding the Universities and schools in which not so long ago Marxism mesmerised so many of the teaching profession and their students. It is not so much an understanding of the strictly military problems of NATO or the statistics of Soviet rearmament that have brought this about. It is the *Gulag Archipelago* and the rest of Alexander Solzhenitzyn's convincing revelations of the systematic oppression of the human spirit by the Soviet regime which television, publishers and press have made known to millions. It is the revulsion caused by one reported example after another of the arrests, trials and imprisonment of the 'dissidents' as they are called in Russia and Czechoslovakia. This flagrant defiance of President Carter's efforts to secure the safeguard of human rights has embedded in the public mind characteristics of the Communist system which were hitherto well known only to a smaller number of well-informed people who remembered the crushing of the Hungarian uprising in 1956 and of the 'Prague Spring' of 1968.

There are many other ways in which the hardships inflicted on their fellow men and women, and particularly their co-religionists, by the Communists in Eastern Europe and South-East Asia, arouse the sympathies of large sections of opinion in the Western World. The Jews and the Baptists in the United States are very much alive to the treatment of their brethren in the Soviet Union, as are members of several Protestant churches to the harassment of their communities in Romania. It is the Roman Catholics who form the bulk of the population in Poland, Lithuania and the Western Ukraine, Czechoslovakia and Hungary who are the most formidable obstacle to atheistic rule and enforced education in the Soviet bloc and who suffer persecution, directed particularly against their clergy and religious orders. An indication of the extent of the solidarity with them which is bestirred in Western countries is the steady increase in donations from individuals and parishes to 'Aid to the Church in Need' which continues to send them help in money and kind — $35.5 million in 1978 — more than half from Germany, France Belgium and Switzerland. The wave of charity evoked in France, the United States, Britain and other countries by the appalling trials of the 'boat people', refugees from Communist rule in Vietnam, is another recent event which has left its mark on many minds. Nor, I think, can one ignore the widespread realisation of the baneful power of the KGB and the crudities of the Communist police state which have furnished the background of a whole generation of fictional literature, some purely sensational, but much of it — of the Le Carré standard — well documented and convincing. None of this, of course, has any direct bearing on the strategic situation. But it all adds up to a considerable volume of hostility to the political system of the Soviet Union which outweighs, in the scales of public opinion, the noisier sentiments of the Russophil Left. This is a fact of the first importance when we consider the increased effort and cost of defence which is bound to confront NATO in the coming years.

It is easier to say what the Atlantic Alliance is against than what it is for. The blatant materialism, the sexual obsession, the flouting of authority at every level, the violence and vandalism, which are so often publicised as features of the 'free world', obscure the sound hearts and basic morality of the American people and of the old European nations, and represent the kind of freedom for which no decent man would risk his life. Freedom from foreign interference is undoubtedly the minimum good which each nation demands; and it is because the Atlantic Alliance exists to protect this and, within the nation, one's own way of life against the totalitarian tyranny of which we have such convincing evidence, that I believe there will be a sufficient foundation of popular support for it as long as that tyranny lasts. I doubt the honesty of going further than this and seeking a kind of common credo for the Allied nations. Dean Achesom at the signing of the North Atlantic Treaty in April 1949, said

> The reality of the Treaty is the unity of belief, of spirit, of interest of the community of nations represented here. It is the product of many centuries of common thought and of the blood of many simple and brave men. . . . The reality lies not in the common pursuit of material good or of a power to dominate others. It lies in the affirmation of moral and spiritual values which govern the kind of life they propose to lead, and which they propose to defend by all possible means should the necessity be thrust upon them.

Unfortunately this kind of uplifting rhetoric, which is characteristic of American public oratory, and reflects an idealism and optimism which warm the heart, rings somewhat hollow today. It is enough to find moral justification for NATO in the old rule of natural law *vim vi repellere omnia jura permittunt.* 'It is always lawful to repel force by force.'

2　Some illusions to be dissipated

THE THIRD WORLD; COLD WAR; *DÉTENTE*

The great matters at issue between the Soviet Union and the non-communist world are so entangled in the current vocabulary of slogans and personified generalisations that it is necessary to take account of their formative influence upon public opinion. It is the arbitrary division of mankind into Left and Right, Progressive and Reactionary, which is the most familiar practice of those whose trade it is to report or comment upon the news. The next stage is the separation of any unfamiliar figures, at least by implication, into 'goodies' and 'baddies'. This has been made the dominant principle of Marxist propaganda, the 'baddies' naturally being conservatives, capitalists, imperialists, all who are opposed to Muscovite policies and, more widely, all who are identified with the existing order of things as against revolutionary change, presented nowadays as 'liberation'. The trial of strength between Communist Russia and the Atlantic Alliance is not immune from this atmosphere.

It was the Spanish Civil War and the emotions which it aroused which first brought about the alignment, which had never existed before in Britain and Western Europe, of liberals, social democrats and pacifists with the communists. Those were the days of the *Front Populaire* and *Le Rassemblement Universel pour la Paix* — the first major effort of the Communist International to exploit the 'Peace Movement' of the West. Briefly interrupted by the Molotov — Ribbentrop Pact, this alliance of sentiment returned so soon as the Nazi invasion of Russia had made the Soviet Union an ally. Among American Democrats, when the United States entered the war, the flirtation became even more fervid, culminating in President Roosevelt's lunatic prophecy after the Yalta Conference in 1944, 'The two great

13

Republics, American and Soviet, standing shoulder to shoulder
will together guarantee the peace and order of the world.'[1]

The disillusionment was complete. In five years the American
Republic found itself arrayed in global antagonism to the Soviet
Republic. But it was not long before the old syren song was heard
again in the West, and the old habit of 'no enemies on the left'
reasserted itself among progressives on both sides of the Atlantic.
In the process, the jargon of Communist propaganda — 'liberation
armies' and 'freedom fighters' for instance — crept into the vocabulary, not only of journalists and broadcasters, but of political
leaders and churchmen. This tendency has given a slant to various
popular slogans and clichés, such as 'Third World', 'Cold War',
and even *'détente'* which is unfavourable to the Atlantic Alliance
as a means of military opposition to the Soviets. It is time to take
them to pieces because of the illusions which they foster.

The Third World

This is one of the silliest of these clichés. Where is it and what
does it mean? The expression was in fact invented by a French
journalist and became part of the stock-in-trade of the media in
the 1950s. It was used to designate *grosso modo* the nations
which were not incorporated in either the Soviet bloc or the
Western Alliance. These were described as *le tiers monde* on the
analogy of *le Tiers Etat*, the Third Estate of French society,
namely the Common People led by the *bourgeoisie*, which came
into its own at the Revolution in contrast to the two privileged
orders, the Aristocracy and the Church. The analogy is a very
forced one (for which of the two great 'blocs' of today corresponds
to the Nobility and which to the Hierarchy of the 1780s?) and is
significant only as an indication of an emotional belief in the
revolutionary potential of the emerging colonial peoples. That
apocalyptic vision, which has had a considerable vogue, inspires
the opening words of Joseph Comblin's *Théologie de la
Revolution*[2], 'The revolution of which we shall speak, is the world
revolution which is beginning to shine on the horizon of this 20th.
century and which nothing, it seems, can prevent exploding in the
21st. century. It is the revolution of the proletariat nations.' This
is the conception of the 'Third World' which so excites the
Progressives; but, in fact, the many states, large and small, which
are outside either the Soviet bloc or the Atlantic Alliance do not

constitute a single source of power. Some, like the great and wealthy states of Latin America — Brazil, Argentina, Mexico and Venezuela — have their own distinctive policies. Of other countries formerly under European rule or protection, the oil-producing states of the Middle East are in an immensely powerful position which their rulers are in no mind to share with the smaller emancipated colonies; and many others — India, Pakistan, Nigeria, the Ivory Coast and Singapore — have problems and aims of their own, which are little affected by their nominal membership of the so-called non-aligned Group. Collectively this, mainly Afro-Asian, group of the decolonised can exert, owing to the unreal voting system of the United Nations, a kind of verbal stranglehold on that institution which more often impedes than promotes any effective decision.

The practical significance of this group which had its origin in the Bandoeng Conference of 1955 is twofold. In the first place it has served, by exploiting a false 'guilt complex' of the former colonial powers, to extract from them and their American allies the maximum financial aid for 'development'. The goodwill of the 'unaligned' governments is sought both by the Soviets and the West, but it is the West that has to pay. There are, of course, genuine links, cultural and otherwise, between European powers and their former dependencies which naturally prompt the economical and technical assistance called for in each case; and, as the Europeans unite, so the European Community, by its Lomé Convention and subsequent agreements with African, Caribbean and Pacific states, co-ordinates the commercial advantages which Europe can offer on a wider scale. American aid, mostly channelled through the World Bank and other United Nations agencies, has been largely associated with the hereditary anti-imperialism of the United States; and the publicity methods employed, such as the wild exaggerations of the Food and Agriculture Organization, have contributed to the over-simple picture of a world crudely divided into the greedy rich and the hungry poor. It is the latter only who are generally meant nowadays by the Third World. It is a picture constantly used to denounce the malice of capitalists. In so far as it stimulates the flow of genuine charity from the churches and the communities of Western Europe and North America to the real centres of human poverty and distress in India, Indo-China, tropical Africa or South America, it has served a very good purpose, though the propaganda of the Left has striven to give a political flavour to the whole operation and the communists have succeeded, in some notorious cases, in diverting funds to assist their sanguinary 'wars of liberation'.

In the second place the non-aligned group, which may be called the political core of the Third World, has provided the Soviet Union with the means of extending, through an international forum, its main strategy outside Europe, which is to exploit anti-colonial sentiments in order to entrench communist influence, wherever the opportunity offers, and so weaken that of the United States and its Allies. We have seen this in action in Vietnam; in bitter rivalry with China in Kampuchea; in all the former Portuguese dependencies; in Southern Arabia; in Ethiopia; in the Caribbean Islands and those of the Indian Ocean. The most ambitious effort to capture the non-aligned movement as a whole for Soviet Communism was the Havana Conference, staged by Fidel Castro, as President of it, in 1979. The very size of the Conference, to which even Spain and Portugal were lured as well as Marshal Tito the original head of the movement, was the undoing of this design, for watered-down resolutions took much of the sting out of the original anti-American texts. It was not long before a substantial minority of non-aligned governments took the initiative in proposing that the United Nations Assembly should demand the immediate withdrawal of Soviet troops from Afghanistan, a demand which received the support of an overwhelming majority. This was a great set-back to the Kremlin, for the Third World had long been one of the routine weapons of Soviet political propaganda against the Atlantic Alliance. Even as early as 1960 NATO had been made a dirty word in Africa.

There are, of course, other meanings of the Third World slogan. In the Argentine, Brazil, Chile and Colombia it is the Third World priests who are the most ardent revolutionaries, some even militant guerrilleros. But their Third World is not a matter of international anti-colonialism; it is the mass of the poor and the under-privileged within their countries whose grievance is against their own governments. But, however different the groups of humanity who are lumped together under this silly title which occurred to a French journalist a quarter of a century ago, they are all assumed to be hostile to capitalism and to be the wards of its political enemy.

The Cold War

The 'Cold War' is another well-worn cliché which often obscures the truth. It was invented to describe a particular episode in the relations between the Communist Party of the Soviet Union and the West. It was the period when Stalin found himself thwarted, after the Communist seizure of Czechoslovakia in 1948, in his attempt to extend his revolutionary Empire in Europe, by the Marshall Plan and the North Atlantic Treaty. The whole world was irreconcilably divided, his henchman, Zhdanor declared, between two 'camps', the Socialist Camp and the American Capitalist Camp; and the Communist Parties throughout the world were committed to an intense war of agitation and subversion against the latter. It was because this campaign fell short of hot, or open, war, in contrast to the violent fighting upon which the Communists were soon engaged in Korea, that it was called the 'Cold War' by the press and radio of the West.

In the next few years, when the violence of the Cominform's propaganda intermittently slackened, as it did already after the Soviet blockade of Berlin was abandoned, the Communists turned round and accused the West of conducting a 'cold war', whenever there was public criticism of Soviet behaviour. So the phrase came to be used by the scriveners and broadcasters of both sides to designate the years, say, 1949 to 1961–2, before the tendency for appeasement became vocal in the West, and before the Party under Nikita Kruschev's leadership committed itself to the more subtle 'Policy of Peaceful Coexistence' (which we shall examine later) as a means of achieving victory without war. Thus, in the popular usage, the term 'Cold War' came to be used to denote both the attitude of active hostility to Communist Russia and a period of past history, like the Middle Ages. So Margaret Thatcher, being outspoken in her views on that subject, was promptly greeted by *Pravda*, when she came to power, as the Iron Lady and the new Cold Warrior. Even more strident was the denunciation of President Carter for reviving the Cold War by the strong measures which he took against the Soviet Union at the beginning of 1980. Nor has President Reagan escaped condemnation.

It is true that the official pursuit of *détente* and the lip-service paid to it, which reached its apogee in the Helsinki Conference on Security and Co-operation in Europe in 1975, created in the minds of the ill-informed majority the impression that, whatever 'noises off' Soviet Russia might make, it was settling down to a more or less normal relationship and was of no particular danger to one's peace of mind. This is particularly true of the French, whose reaction to Soviet policy has always been low-keyed and distrustful of wordy warfare. Until the return of eyeball to eyeball confrontation between Washington and Moscow in 1980, it was possible for the superficial observer to treat the 'Cold War' as a thing of the past.

But no serious student could hold that the temporary reduction of polemics indicated any change in the aggressive nature of Soviet strategy. In so far as there was a suspension of verbal warfare, it was very one-sided, particularly during the last few years of the SALT II negotiations, when a cautious optimism was the order of the day in the United States and regard for Soviet susceptibilities the rule. But on the Soviet side hostile propaganda against other Western countries never ceased. For instance, abuse of British policies in Africa and Northern Ireland and the highlighting of strikes in the United Kingdom, as a consequence of the supposed oppression of the working class, were constant features of it. More important than words were the visible acts of the Soviet Government during the last decade, from its incessant and unprecedented increase of armaments to its territorial interventions, with its own or surrogate revolutionary troops in Africa. Nor could there have been a more flagrant defiance of NATO than the Portuguese Revolution, engineered by the Communist Party most closely identified with Soviet direction of any in Europe, which, despite political reverses in the metropolis, resulted in all the overseas provinces falling, as planned, into Communist hands. It was doubtful whether, after Afghanistan, relations between Moscow and Washington could once again be susceptible to reasonable negotiation. Cold War would be a euphemism for the international atmosphere which that dangerous adventure created in the first quarter of 1980.

Détente

This, on the available evidence, killed the state of mind and the hopes described as *détente*, so far as the two super powers are concerned. It is, however, necessary to make a serious study of the subject. For it was soon clear that a great part on the non-Communist world, including Atlantic Alliance governments and representative bodies of opinion, though deploring the Soviet military aggression, was most reluctant to give up the advantages of peaceful trade and exchanges with the Socialist countries of Europe.

Détente is the most potent of the slogans which have confused the public view of the Soviet Union in the non-Communist world. It was introduced into the vocabulary of diplomacy in 1966 by Monsieur Harmel, the Belgian Foreign Minister, at a meeting of the North Atlantic Council, and two years later was formalised by the Council as an objective of its policy, as well as its primary purpose of deterring military aggression. Etymologically the meaning of the French word, for which there is no exact equivalent in Russian, and none in English, is exactly the opposite of what these gentlemen intended: it means the release of tension in the spring of a pistol by pulling the trigger which fires the shot. As a political term, *détente* implies a process of reducing the tension or attitude of mutual hostility between the Atlantic Alliance and the Warsaw Pact in Europe; and for this purpose NATO suggested the 'balanced reduction' of the forces confronting one another. It was five years before the Soviet Government saw the advantage of taking up this suggestion, and another two before negotiations started in Vienna between certain of the Atlantic Allies and of the Soviet bloc in Europe. Though some progress was gradually made towards a possible phased withdrawal of American and Russian manpower, negotiations were paralysed by the events of December 1979 and January 1980.

President Johnson, meanwhile, had suggested to the Soviets in 1964 a bilateral discussion of the possibility of limiting the number of intercontinental nuclear missiles. Three years later Mr Kosygin agreed to the idea, and there began the long-drawn Strategic Arms Limitation Talks, of which the second instalment (SALT II) was a complicated treaty, frozen at the beginning of 1980 in the United States Senate, because of the sense of outrage caused by the Soviet invasion of Afghanistan.

So far then, except for some minor agreements designed to limit the scope of nuclear weapons, such as the Non-Proliferation Treaty and another precluding the placing of nuclear explosive devices on the sea-bed, there had, despite interminable discussions, been no practical result of the initiative taken by the West for the reduction of armaments. All that the SALT agreements really amounted to was the attempted codification of a stalemate between the two nuclear super power, which would no doubt be better than unlimited rivalry. In the process the passage of time has radically altered the data of negotiations. In the 1960s there was a rough balance of conventional forces between the two sides in Europe; now, except for the navies, the Warsaw Pact has achieved an absolute superiority over NATO. At that time also the United States had a far more powerful armoury of nuclear war heads than the Soviets — witness the swift end of the Cuban missile crisis; now the two super powers have a numerical equivalence in their weapon of mass destruction, but with the technical advantages tilting to the Soviet side.

But if the original intention of reducing tension between the rival alliances by the tangible means of reducing armaments has been a complete failure, the psychological and political consequences of the official commitment to *détente* have been very great in the Western world. Among the peoples of the Atlantic Alliance it responds to the deeply-rooted desire for peace and stability, and for deliverance from a condition of permanent hostility, inherent in rival military alliances but unnatural to all who share the legacy of the Christian civilisation. For this reason alone governments are obliged to pursue *détente*, even though it be a will o' the wisp. Attitudes vary, of course, from the basic optimism of the Americans, who cannot see that their own ideals are not mirrored in the objectives of the other side, to the fear of their powerful neighbour in the smaller states of Northern Europe, while Russophil sentiments are present in lesser or greater degree among the parties of the Left in all European countries. Hence the wealth of wishful thinking about co-operation with Communist Russia along the road to an earthly paradise. It is a complete illusion. The Soviet view of *détente* is very different. Not stability but the communist rule of the world is the ultimate aim. We shall study in a later chapter the present state and probable evolution of Soviet foreign policy as a whole. Here it will suffice to say that, having looked this Western gift-horse in the mouth with little enthusiasm for five or six years, it occurred to the Soviet leaders and to Mr Brezhnev in particular that *détente* could be a useful instrument of the 'Policy of Peaceful Coexistence' which remains, since 1961, an essential part of the Programme of the CPSU. Its relation to that Policy is defined as follows by Lord Brimelow.

The Soviet doctrine of peaceful coexistence as struggle is primary, strategic and comprehensive; Soviet statements about *détente* are secondary, tactical and partial.[3]

The essential passage of the programme of the Party reads;

Peaceful coexistence serves as the basis for peaceful competition between socialism and capitalism on an international scale and constitutes a specific form of class struggle between them. ... Peaceful coexistence affords more favourable opportunities for the struggle of the working class in the capitalist countries and facilitates the struggle of the peoples of the colonial and dependent countries for their liberation.

While there is much else in the programme to win liberal applause, it is important to realise that the 'liberation' of colonial and dependent peoples is regarded as an essential object of the policy of peaceful coexistence. In fact the wars of the last two decades, with the exception of the Arab—Israeli war and the conflict between Iraq and Iran, have almost all been conducted by communist 'liberation movements' sponsored by the USSR and fought with Soviet arms. Of these the most costly in human life and suffering — and humiliation to the United States — was the Vietnam War itself, shortly to be followed by the attempted conquest of Cambodia. Meanwhile thirteen years of fighting by Soveit-aided insurgents in Portuguese Africa culminated in the still unfinished attempt to conquer Angola with the aid of Cuban troops, transported and armed by the Soviet Union in support of the Communist MPLA. There followed the arming and training of the so-called 'Patriotic Front' guerrillas operating from Mozambique and Zambia to attack Rhodesia, of the SWAPO to attack Namibia from Angola, and the Communist Yemeni to harass Saudi Arabia and Oman. An airlift of Soviet, Cuban and East German troops to complete the communist control of Ethiopia ensued. Yet throughout these bloodstained years, the United States and its allies — until the Afghanistan strike — continued to maintain the fiction that the Soviet Union was committed, as they were, to *détente*. There was indeed a sorrowful little protest by the North Atlantic Council at the Angolan intervention, and a more vigorous reaction from Henry

Kissinger, until then the major prophet of *détenté*. Speaking on 3 February 1976 at San Francisco, he said

> As the United States strives to shape a more hopeful world, it can never forget that global stability and security rest upon the equilibrium between the great Powers. If the Soviet Union is permitted to exploit opportunities arising out of local conflicts by military means, the hopes we have to progress towards a more peaceful international order will ultimately be undermined. . . . Let no nation believe that Americans will long remain indifferent to the despatch of expeditionary forces and vast supplies of arms to impose minority governments, especially when they come from a nation in the Western hemisphere.

This was, in the event, a futile gesture. President Brezhnev replied three weeks later

> Some bourgeois politicians affect astonishment and make a fuss about the solidarity of Soviet Communists and of the Soviet people with the struggle of other peoples for freedom and progress. This is either naiveté or more probably, deliberate obfuscation. For it is as clear as can be that *détente* and peaceful coexistence relate to *inter-state relations*. . . . *Détente* in no way rescinds or can rescind the class struggle. None can count on Communists, in conditions of *détente*, resigning themselves to capitalist exploitation.

It was not till the Soviet invasion of Afghanistan — also undertaken ostensibly in support of an indigenous rising — that President Carter bestirred himself, not only to denounce that military aggression, but to take practical steps to demonstrate American abhorrence of it.

It seemed, for a moment as if that would be the end of *détente*. The aged Politburo in Moscow appeared to have come to the conclusion that the strategic advantages of military expansion in the key area of the Middle East, in which Egypt had now joined the American 'camp', outweighed the more subtle benefits derived from *détente*, understimating the anger of the hitherto harmless American President. In the West *détente* with Soviet Russia was written off as the illusion which it had proved to be by most political leaders and publicists in the USA and Britain, but not in Germany, France and other allied countries, though the Soviets' aggression against an independent state was universally reprobated. The bulk of the West German population, the most important component of NATO in Europe, concurred in the general verdict, but the practical advantages of the 1971 agreement on Berlin and the *Ostpolitik*, which achieved the normalisation of relations with East Germany, the Soviet Union, Poland and Czechoslovakia, remain for them a compelling argument against any avoidable widening of the rift between East and West. In France the Communist Party decided to support the Soviets' intervention while the government, though condemning it, was unwilling to undo its traditional attachment to *détente*.

Besides these national differences we have to take account of the edifice of bureaucracy created in thirty-five states of Europe and North America to follow up the Helsinki Conference on Security and Co-operation in Europe, which was the culmination of President Brezhnev's endeavour to internationalise his peaceful co-existence policy, and the basketful of resolutions which it produced. The burden of the long-drawn, inconclusive haggling at the first follow-up conference at Belgrade fell mostly upon the diplomats of the states concerned, as it has done in 1980 again at Madrid, and aroused very little interest in the European media of information. But the United States Government and almost every citizens' organisation concerned with civil rights or the defence of minorities in that country took the matter very seriously. For them the Final Act of Helsinki meant exclusively the undertakings to safeguard human rights, the item to which the Soviet Union attached the least importance. President Carter's attempts to secure respect for these rights in the Communist states having proved a complete failure, the American Commission on Security and Co-operation in Europe embarked, with the help of the 'Helsinki WATCH committees', set up in Washington and New York on the model of the hapless monitoring committees, in Moscow, Prague and Warsaw, on an exhaustive examination of conscience concerning 'US Compliance with Human Rights'.[4] I have no doubt that migrant workers, American Indians and other underprivileged people will benefit; but this is a consequence of *détente* far removed from our subject. From the point of view of the Soviet bloc the most practical and useful parts of the Helsinki Conference proposals were the extensive and detailed provisions for the supply to the states represented of all sorts of industrial products and technology. This gave a substantial impetus to the export to Soviet Russia of such machines, inventions and know-how from the United States, Britain, France, Germany and Japan, which was already considerable.

3 The strategic situation transformed

The strategic situation in which the trial of strength between the Communist Party of the Soviet Union, with its allies, and the United States, with its allies, continues in the 1980s is very different from what it was in 1949 or 1954. Indeed, if a defensive alliance of the latter were formed today, it could hardly be the same as the very restricted North Atlantic Treaty with which we have lived for thirty years. The adaptation of the old model to today's realities is not without difficulty.

The two most obvious facts which are altering the strategic situation of the Atlantic Alliance for the worse are the military superiority of the Warsaw Pact's conventional forces and the global character of the Soviet Navy. The significance of these developments will emerge from our analyses of the armed strength of the rival groups in Parts Two and Three of this book. Here I propose to study two other factors which have contributed to transform the balance of power, the recent developments of nuclear arms as they affect Europe and the extension of Soviet political and military power outside Europe.

NUCLEAR DEVELOPMENTS IN EUROPE

The new situation was described very clearly by Professor Laurence Martin in his broadcast talk 'A Dangerous Imbalance' in November 1979.[1]

The snag is that the North Atlantic Treaty was signed in 1949, in an almost pre-nuclear world, before the Soviet Union had tested a nuclear weapon, before the H or thermo-nuclear bomb had even become feasible, before the intercontinental missile had been developed. Thus the vital American

25

guarantee was issued before the United States itself had
become vulnerable. Ever since that vulnerability emerged,
there has been a question-mark over an alliance in which the
main centre of power — almost, if not quite, the only centre of
nuclear power — is widely separated from the likely sites of
aggression. What is happening today is that the overall rise in
Soviet military power is making the Soviet capability for local
aggression more credible, while simultaneously Soviet strategic
nuclear power makes the American contribution to escalation
more doubtful.

The American guarantees, to which Professor Martin refers,
were simply the assumption that, in fulfilling its obligation under
Article 5 of the North Atlantic Treaty, the United States in
common with its Allies would use its available military resources
to defeat an aggressor. While the nuclear arm was not specified,
the United States and, in a smaller way, the United Kingdom,
were the only powers able to employ the 'atom bomb' as a military
weapon; it was, therefore, assumed that it would, if necessary, be
used.

The rapid development of the weapon by the Americans, since
the destruction of Hiroshima and Nagasaki four years before,
was, from the first, taken to mean that this overwhelming
instrument of mass destruction[2] would give the Atlantic Alliance
an inbuilt superiority over the Soviet Union, itself sufficient to
deter Stalin from risking a further advance in Europe. The moral
and political problems involved had not, I think, been worked out
at the time. It was only when the Soviets were found to be
producing their own thermo-nuclear weapons, and the
Americans for the first time felt 'under the gun' that the threat of
using it in instant retaliation for a first nuclear strike became an
accepted part of United States and, consequently NATO
strategy. In fact, the defensive barrier which General Eisenhower
so quickly built up in 1951, when the European Command was
first established, consisted exclusively of 'conventional forces'
based upon the existing United States, British and French land
and air Occupation Forces in Germany and the units which their
Canadian and European Allies agreed to earmark for the
purpose. At sea, NATO depended similarly upon the co-
operation in the Atlantic, the Channel and the Mediterranean of
the existing navies of signatories of the treaty, none of whose

vessels were equipped for nuclear warfare.

Until the late 1960s, the military affairs of NATO and public debate about the cost of them were, so far as the Europeans were concerned, almost entirely related to the number and quality of manpower and material. Strategic nuclear arms were the business of the United States, Britain's 'independent nuclear deterrent' was the financial and political peculiarity of the United Kingdom, though its nuclear bombing force was committed in principle to NATO. The French nuclear 'force de frappe' as it developed, was exclusively intended for the defence of France. The only nuclear equipment with which NATO's forces in Europe were latterly concerned consisted of some 7000 relatively small tactical nuclear weapons supplied by the United States and stored in certain dumps in Germany. They could only be used (e.g. by German, or British as well as US forces) on the 'double key system', that is, with the express permission of the President of the United States. But no practical plan for using them has ever been officially devised. In short, however serious the competition in nuclear missiles of Soviet Russia, it was taken for granted that the United States had the necessary superiority in quantity and quality to cope with it. As Henry Kissinger candidly observed: 'The secret dream of every European was, of course, to avoid a nuclear war but, secondly, if there had to be a nuclear war, to have it conducted over their heads by the strategic forces of the United States and the Soviet Union.'[3]

The psychological consequences of this habitual dependence for national security upon a 'God in the machine' several thousand miles away has been very serious and is likely, for years to come, to impede the whole-hearted co-operation of the European Allies in strengthening NATO's capacity to deter or defeat an offensive move by the Warsaw Pact. In the United Kingdom, to take an example, 'defence on the cheap' was characteristic of all the governments, Labour and Conservative, from 1957 to 1977. The White Paper on Defence of 1957, contending that the American nuclear power was the primary protection of Europe, reduced the United Kingdom's contribution — apart from its strategic bomber force — to help in providing a trip-wire of conventional forces on the Continent. To reduce defence expenditure thereafter became the main concern of the Labour Party. By 1975, the British Government's reductions, aimed at limiting the cost of defence to four and a half per cent[4] of the GNP provoked a serious remonstrance from NATO. 'The changes of special concern are the reduction of reinforcement capability in the Northern and Southern regions; the removal of naval and air forces from the Mediterranean, and the decline of maritime capabilities in the Eastern Atlantic and Channel areas.' The Dutch Socialist Party, at the same time, were demanding their country's withdrawal from NATO unless its tactical nuclear weapons were included in the proposed Mutual Force reductions. The Danes, having reduced their period of national service to nine months, were proposing further cuts in their defence budget.

It was not until July 1977 that American pressure and an awakening to the threat of the Warsaw Pact's massive rearmament induced all members of the Atlantic Alliance to agree to an all-round increase of three per cent in their real defence expenditure;[5] it was not until 1978 that the outcome of the SALT II negotiations, as they have become known, focused attention upon two facts of over-riding importance. The first was that American superiority in strategic nuclear weapons was a thing of the past; the second was that the Soviets had developed a series of powerful nuclear missiles, excluded from the SALT Treaty because they are not inter-continental in range, which could destroy any city in Western Europe. Though each of the Super-powers would dispose of some 2400 land- and sea-launched ballistic missiles, it was believed by critics of the treaty that the heavy and accurate Soviet ICBMs could knock out the American *Minutemen* in their fixed silos in a first strike; while the United States ICBMs were designed for the mass destruction of centres of population. And it came to be realised that, except in retaliation against a devastating attack, it would be morally and politically almost impossible for an American President to order the launching of the ultimate weapon. What would be quite impossible would be for him to order it as a warning of an attack in Europe, with the destruction of, say, New York or Chicago as the inevitable consequence. The Soviets, realising these inhibitions but having no such scruples of their own about using nuclear weapons to subdue Europe, have produced and deployed a whole series of intermediate nuclear arms clearly intended for that purpose, the most formidable of which are the mobile SS 20s fitted with three separate warheads (MIRVs) (each much more devastating than the Hiroshima bomb), and the supersonic

Backfire bomber capable of launching nuclear bombs upon any target in Europe.

It was to counter this immediate threat within the European theatre that the Pentagon devised, in agreement with the Nuclear Planning Committee of NATO, the plan of stationing in certain of the European Allies' territories a series of nuclear weapons, operated by US personnel and capable of reaching targets in European Russia — namely, 108 of the Pershing missile launchers adapted to the necessary range, and 464 of the air-breathing, low-flying and accurate cruise missiles in which the United States has a certain advantage over the Soviets. The German Federal Republic agreed to have the Pershing 2s on its territory and the United Kingdom and Italy to have the cruise missiles stationed on theirs. The Dutch and Belgians for internal reasons have boggled at collaborating. This, so far from being an abandonment of their European allies by the Americans is, in fact, a far more realistic contribution to their defence than is dependence upon the intercontinental weapons of mass destruction; and I am bound to say, the same contention applies to the British and French SLBMs of similar calibre, as the proposed Trident missiles would be. The speculation is that it would be possible by these means to counteract, if not deter, the Soviets' use of nuclear devices in the European theatre without recourse on either side to the ultimate strategic arms. Only if the Soviets were to resort to their intercontinental heavy-weights would the final escalation result. It is a gamble; but it might succeed.

We have seen[6] with what difficulty even a qualified concurrence in this plea by the North European Allied governments was reached in the North Atlantic Council in December 1979, and the anxiety of the Germans not to endanger thereby the fruit of their *Ostpolitik*. The same unwillingness to provoke Soviet hostility was seen in the reaction of the same and other countries to the United States desire for co-operation in responding to the Soviet occupation of Afghanistan. France, in both cases, keeping her powder dry and, unwilling to disturb her long-standing liaison with Russia, left the decision to others. The trouble is that in countries habitually committed to the illusion of *détente* and the accompanying Socialist addiction to the progressive reduction of armaments, large numbers of people continue to live in the cloud-cuckoo-land of yesterday without waking up to the new nuclear situation and its dangers.

SOVIET POLITICAL AND MILITARY POWER OUTSIDE EUROPE

The most striking way in which the balance of power in the world has changed since the early years of the Atlantic Treaty is the replacement of Western by Soviet control of areas of great strategic and economic importance in Asia and Africa. It is mainly, but not entirely, the result of the Soviet Union filling the vacuum created by decolonisation, that is the liquidation of the European empires.

There have indeed been important exceptions to this process. The countries of the Indian sub-continent, subject to rival Chinese and Soviet influences, have contrived so far to remain 'non-aligned', as have Thailand, the Philippines and the other ASEAN states. In the Middle East the good relations of Egypt and Saudi Arabia with the United States and Oman's treaty with the United Kingdom mitigate the general coldness to the West of the Arab countries and the nervousness of the Gulf Sultanates. In the Far East the rise of Japan to a great place in the economy of the world, and its friendship, notwithstanding its diplomatic independence, with the Western Allies is their one major extra-European asset of the last two decades, added to their common interest with China in resisting Soviet 'hegemony'. In Africa, while the majority of the former colonies are powerfully influenced by Soviet Communism, Morocco and Tunisia in the North, the Ivory Coast and Senegal in the West, Zaire in the Centre and Kenya in the East have remained relatively stable and independent. The trend of politics in the former Caribbean colonies seemed to be the advance of Marxism under Cuban influence, though the defeat of the left in the Jamaican Election marked a turning of the tide. Martinique and Guadeloupe remain Departments of the French Republic, as does Reunion in the Indian Ocean. Hong Kong continues, at the goodwill of the Chinese People's Republic, as a British Crown Colony *sui generis*, wealthy and overcrowded.

But when every allowance has been made for favourable exceptions to the general loss of influence by the Western Allies in the decolonised world and the good relations which they have cultivated with parts of it — notably between France and Belgium and their former dependencies — there can be no denying the formidable gains of the Soviet Union. Of these the most substantial have been in the former French Indo-China, in the former Portuguese Africa and, mostly at the expense of British influence, in the Horn of Africa and the adjoining Red Sea area.

The victory of the Communist Vietcong over the Americans was an event of lasting and baneful significance. The hitherto invincible North American Republic, though employing every device of modern warfare except the nuclear arm, had been defeated, with the loss of 55 000 dead and hundreds of thousands of wounded, by an Asian Marxist 'Liberation Movement', armed and supported with an intensive propaganda campaign by the Soviet Union, of which it is now the recognised ally. Much has been written about the traumatic consequences of this disaster upon the American people. More important is its psychological effect throughout the world in weakening confidence in American power and capacity for leadership, an effect which the subsequent crisis of Presidential authority and a period of erratic diplomacy did nothing to dispel.

Of greater strategic significance — since the United States Pacific fleet and the Chinese presence can mitigate to some extent the inconvenience of a Soviet satellite in South-East Asia — is the control by Communists of the Muscovite allegiance of all the former Portuguese dependencies in, and off the coasts of Africa. These are the Cape Verde Islands, with the large airport of Sul, Guinea Bissau, Angola, Mozambique, and the islands of São Tomé and Principe in the Gulf of Guinea. The important harbours of Luanda, Lobito (terminus of the British-owned Benguela Railway) and Mocamede on the Atlantic coast, Mabuto, Beira and Nacala on the western coast of the Indian Ocean, with the modern airfields of Angola and Mozambique, provide every facility for naval or air interception of the stream of tankers and merchantmen sailing around Africa to and from Western Europe. These ports are also the main outlets for the export of copper from Zambia and Zaire and of many valuable minerals, strategic and otherwise, produced in Angola and Zimbabwe. Mabuto (Laurenco Marques) also handles important exports from South Africa and all the iron from Swaziland, while Nacala is Malawi's only outlet to the sea.

The Soviet control of the former Portuguese Provinces, in all of which Communist governments are installed, having treaties of alliance and mutual defence with the Soviet Union, is the outcome of a classical case of long-range Communist planning, complete with the creation and seizure of opportunities, from 1960 to 1974, which the rulers of the Western 'democracies' were unable to understand and counteract. The key to its success was the intense 'Liberation' propaganda campaign which made skilful and unscrupulous use of anti-imperialist and pro-Black sentiments in the United States, the emotional legacy of the old anti-slavery campaign of the Non-Conformist conscience in England, the Left-wing lurch of the Roman Catholic Church since the Vatican Council, and the anti-colonial obsession of the United Nations. There was in fact no objective basis for this atrocity-mongering campaign in Portuguese Africa, nor was there at any time any popular rising against the Portuguese. Indeed, their success in countering the small Communist-led terrorist/liberation groups with mainly indigenous armed forces for thirteen years and advancing important economic develop- ment — especially of Angola — in the process, was remarkable. But the prospects of the Salazar regime holding out for its old imperial responsibilities *contra mundum* were so evidently precarious, and the strategic consequences in Africa of its political collapse — foreseen by well-informed observers — so serious for the West, that the American and British governments of the time did these countries and NATO a poor service in taking no action to forestall them. The fact is that they never took seriously the Communists' plan of campaign. The Western Intelligence Services, for instance, were well aware of the pro- gramme adopted by the Portuguese Communist Party at its Congress in September 1965 at Prague for precipitating the Revolution, and, with it, the takeover of the Overseas Provinces, through the use of well-prepared cadres in the armed forces. The outcome might have been very different if the Americans, supported by Britain, the traditional ally of Portugal, had used all their political, diplomatic and financial influences to induce Dr Caetano's government in Lisbon to expedite, by a genuine process of self-determination, the inevitable independence of the African provinces, to whose autonomy they were already committed.

For Britain the immediate consequences of the Portuguese collapse was, of course, to open the borders of its recalcitrant Rhodesian colony to attack by insurgents, using Communist Mozambique as their base, an operation in which the other neighbouring African states, Angola, Zambia and Botswana joined, with Mr Nyerere of Tanzania cheering from the touchline. The headmen of these countries were soon nicknamed 'Front-line Presidents' by journalists, the 'Front-line' being understood to be that of the African Liberation War against white imperialism. And the real objective of that campaign, in which the liberals of the Western world found themselves in alliance with the Organisation of African Unity and the Soviet Union, was and is the white-ruled Union of South Africa, Namibia and Zimbabwe being but stages on the march. There may be little to choose — from the point of view of its inhabitants — between a Marxist and a Boer dictatorship; what does give us cause for alarm is the dependence of the West upon South Africa for many of its vital raw materials. The most striking strategic success of the Communists' liberation campaign, with their cynical championship of the Africans' human rights against *apartheid*, is that it scared off the British and Americans from the use of Simonstown and from co-operation with South Africa in the naval and air protection of the Cape shipping route.

In addition to the advantages derived from control of the extensive ex-Portuguese territories, the Communists have profited by their presence in the African Unity organisation to bring under their rule the great island of Madagascar — erstwhile French — with its good naval harbour of Diego Suarez and the Comoran Islands, except for Mayotte. The same formula has given the Soviet Union a privileged footing in Mauritius, where their intelligence-gathering fishing trawlers are serviced, and the Seychelles. In North-East Africa the Soviets' first decision to develop Berbera in Somalia as a naval and air base was exchanged for the ambitious policy of bringing the more important prize of Ethiopia firmly within the Socialist Empire. This was accomplished by an airlift of more troops, Cuban, East German and Russian, and heavy equipment than were used to promote the Communist conquest of Angola. This opened the Ethiopian Red Sea ports — not controlled by the Eritrean insurgents — to Soviet shipping. On the eastern approaches to the Straits of Bab el Mandeb the former British colony of Aden has become a Soviet naval and military stronghold, equipped with submarine pens and the latest communication devices; and the 'People's Democratic Republic of Yemen', of which it is the main town, is the basis for Communist military and political intervention in Southern Arabia. The occupation of Afghanistan to the east of the Arabian Gulf has suggested the design of a pincer movement to secure control of the Gulf with its vital importance to the production and transport of oil — a sufficient explanation of the angry reaction which it produced in Washington.

It is difficult to find, apart from a few developments mentioned at the start of this chapter, any advantages outside Europe which have accrued to the Western Allies during the period of decolonisation, which synchronises with the life of the North Atlantic Treaty, to compensate for the strategic gains of the Soviet Union in Africa and Asia. It does not, of course, follow that the rapid extension of the Soviets' political and military influence over so many theoretically independent indigenous states means the inevitable denial of their resources to non-Communist powers. There are not lacking, for instance, in the Foreign Offices and universities of the West, those who argue that the need of normal trade and communication strengthens the case for maintaining *détente* with the USSR. The oil of Cabindu is an example. It is more realistic to conclude that in the event of war (for which NATO is bound to prepare) the consequences to Britain and the other countries of Western and Northern Europe of the interdiction of the oil, minerals and other raw materials upon which their economies largely depend, would be disastrous, and for the United States and Canada very serious. The task of protecting maritime communications is now, as we shall see, a much more difficult task for our navies. There can be no doubt that the strategic balance has been severely tilted to the detriment of the Atlantic Allies.

4   The myth of the Tropic of Cancer

Cancer, the Crab, is one of the signs of the Zodiac which, the encyclopaedias inform us, have a certain mythical as well as seasonal significance. But the mythical character of the Tropic of Cancer in the sphere of world strategy is of a different order; it belongs to a world of make-believe and wishful thinking which supposes that modern war can be confined by lines on a map. The fact that the Tropic of Cancer is legally the southern limit of what is called 'the Treaty Area' of the North Atlantic Treaty is striking evidence of the very different conditions which obtained in 1949 from those which confront us in the 1980s.

At that time the Union of Soviet Socialist Republics, beginning its attempt to break out, in the name of the World Revolution, from the borders of the old Russian Empire, was, essentially a land power. The United States, on the other hand, which aimed to contain that expansion, enjoyed a marked superiority of sea power, to which the Royal Navy made no mean contribution. The first problem, therefore, for the Americans and the British, with the aid of France, Canada, and a number of smaller states which were recovering from the German occupation, and had escaped that of the Soviet Union, was to stop the advance of the Red Army on the European Continent. The Soviet fleets were not impressive, nor were Soviet air forces outside Europe. Neither of these forces had the bases or refuelling stations which were available to the Americans in the Atlantic and the Pacific and those which were still operative in the remaining British and French Empires. Portugal, the traditional ally of England, provided a useful addition, particularly in the Azores, to their naval facilities. On the Soviet side there was one naval development against which it was considered necessary to take precautions, namely the building up of a flotilla of submarines in the Kola inlet near Murmansk, with ice-free access to the North Atlantic.

The Tropic of Cancer, which runs just beyond the southermost point of the east coast of the United States, was judged to be about the furthest that these Soviet boats could patrol, and beyond which no hostile action need be anticipated. It was therefore agreed to include in the new Security Treaty as *casus belli* any attacks north of that line upon ships and aircraft of the signatories of the Atlantic Treaty as well as upon their territories. When Greece and Turkey joined the Alliance — Italy was an original member — this provision was extended to the Mediterranean Sea.

The Tropic of Cancer had the additional advantage, in the context of American politics, of leaving the United States free from any obligation to defend the British colonial Empire, for which Congress had no liking. Most of the French African dependencies were also outside the new treaty area, but Algeria was at that time an integral part of the French Republic.

The progressive liquidation of the British, French, Belgian and Portuguese empires has made these particular considerations irrelevant, replacing them with others. But among the North European signatories of the Atlantic Treaty there are a number of quite different political considerations which have contributed to make their rigid insistence upon the restricted Treaty Area a serious impediment to the efficiency of NATO in the 1980s. It is the rule of unanimity which enables the representative of the Netherlands, Norway and Denmark, in particular, to block any collective action by the North Atlantic Council to protect the Allies' maritime lines of communication and sources of energy outside the limits of the Treaty Area against molestation by the Soviets' powerful navy, now operating in every ocean, and their growing air power. As we shall see, this does not prevent the United States and at least two other Atlantic Allies, Britain and France, from taking steps to defend their interests, as best they may, in the Indian Ocean or the South Atlantic. Naval intelligence is pooled at NATO; but, for all that, it is a great inconvenience for the Military Committee not to be able to plan and direct the action of the Alliance as a whole to cope with the global challenge of Soviet power.

It is the 'limited liability' attitude of certain of the lesser Allies, of which their refusal to contemplate any co-operation outside the Treaty Area is symbolic, which is a source of moral weakness to NATO as an instrument for the corporate defence of the West;

and the Soviet government well knows how to take advantage of it.

While there are in both the Scandinavian states and in the Netherlands many people, including able military men, who are wholly committed to active resistance to aggression, there is a large body of opinion in each whose idea of national policy is to do the minimum required to win American protection in an emergency without provoking the anger of Moscow. This is a common feature — *mutatis mutandis* — of the Socialist parties in Western Europe, with the exception of a majority of the SPD in Germany, the Moderate Right of the British Labour Party and most of the French Socialists, who accept the peculiarly nationalist defence policy of their country. But it is the Left-wing of the British Labour Party which has most influence with its neighbours in the north of Europe.

There are other elements peculiar to the history of these countries which operate against any keenness for defence. Denmark, Norway (which separated from it in 1905) and the Netherlands have a strong tradition of neutrality. Since the 'Wars of the Duchies' of Denmark against Austria and Prussia in 1864, none of these have been involved in hostilities, from the end of the Napoleonic Wars until Hitler's sudden attacks of 1940 which brought them under total German occupation. A hankering to return to neutrality is therefore very natural. Such indeed was one of the objects of the Nordic Council which in the years immediately following the Second World War was being formed around neutral Sweden for the purpose of economic and cultural co-operation between all the Scandinavian countries.

When Denmark's adherence to the projected North Atlantic Treaty was being sought by the United States and Britain in 1949, there was substantial opposition to it from the advocates of the Nordic policy. It was overcome, largely thanks to a vigorous campaign undertaken by a group of Danes, both Conservatives and Socialists, who had distinguished themselves in the Resistance Movement against the Nazis. They called themselves 'the Danish Association for the Atlantic Pact and Democracy'; it was the first of the national citizens' organisations in the Allied countries which were to form a few years later the Atlantic Treaty Association. But disinclination to face up to the military and financial requirements of a defensive Alliance is a perennial feature of Danish politics. I have mentioned the reduction in the period of military service to nine months in the early 1970s; an even greater reduction was proposed even in the tense atmosphere of 1979. It is not long since the maverick Progress Party gained votes at the expense of the Liberals and Social Democrats with its proposals to abolish income tax and national defence, and install an automatic telephone service to Moscow, answering 'We surrender'. That, of course, was an absurd expression of a national weakness, which has to be contrasted to the serious Danish naval co-operation in the defence of the Baltic Approaches and the devotion of the Danish Home Guard.

Norway's political past is distinguished by the fact that the Socialist Party, which dominated the Storting for more than thirty years, was itself a member of the Third International from whence the Russian Bolsheviks emerged.

Between the wars fraternal relations with the Communist Party of the Soviet Union were kept up. Though membership of the Atlantic Alliance, to whose purpose the Norwegians have responded with more virility than their Danish neighbours, of course, put an end to that connection, a particular regard for Russian defensive susceptibilities remains. Hence the undertaking — unique in the Alliance — given to Moscow that no foreign military bases are to be established on Norwegian territory. This greatly increases the difficulties of NATO in planning the aid which can be given to the defence of this huge country which has, in the far north, a land frontier with the Soviet Union, as we shall see when we come to study the problems of NATO's northern front. One justification for the 'Nordic Balance' is that it preserves not only Swedish neutrality but also the precarious degree of independence at present enjoyed by Finland *vis-à-vis* the Soviet Union.

In the Netherlands, whose military contribution to the defence of the Central Front of NATO in Germany is important, a distinguishing feature of the national attitude is the pacifist tradition. The Hague Conferences at the beginning of this century were the first great endeavour to save international peace from the clash of rival alliances which led to the First World War; and the World Court of International Justice meets in the Peace Palace there. A powerful anti-militarist, and particularly anti-nuclear movement has developed in both the Calvinist and Catholic Churches, a movement which spills over into Belgium. Hence the insistence in the Dutch Parliament upon subordinating the modernisation of

NATO's nuclear armoury in Europe to a renewed effort at making an arms limitation agreement with the Soviet Union.

There is a further form of popular emotion that has created an instinctive hostility in the Netherlands and all the Scandinavian countries to any suggestion of a defensive commitment outside the strict Treaty limit of the North Atlantic. It is the result of the impassioned anti-colonial liberation campaign to which I have referred in an earlier chapter. It was the war in Vietnam, or rather the intense Communist propaganda about it, which first transformed the attitude of the students in the University of Oslo from the warm friendship with the United States, which had hitherto been characteristic of the younger generation in Norway, to extreme hostility. The same transformation was soon true also, not only of students, but of a considerable section of public opinion in all Scandinavia, with the then Prime Minister of Sweden, Mr Olof Palme, conducting the orchestra. No sooner had the Vietnam agitation abated with the end of the war against 'American imperialism' than the heat was switched on to Africa with persistent appeals to aid to Communist-led 'Liberation Movements' against the Portuguese, Rhodesia and South Africa. Propaganda on this subject had even more success in the Netherlands, where national committees of respected burghers and clergymen, including even members of the Royal Family, solemnly set about boycotting Angolan coffee. The practical effect of this emotionalism upon the large Left-wing political parties of these countries was certainly to reduce the popularity of NATO as an American and capitalist alliance; and, of course, any suggestion of extending around the African coasts the political and naval activities of NATO beyond the Tropic of Cancer, to counteract the threat to its communications and mineral resources, was anathema.

Such are the particular political and psychological characteristics of three states members of the Atlantic Alliance, whose governments and political parties attach more practical importance than others to *détente* and the resolutions of the Helsinki Conference on Security and Co-operation in Europe, and are particularly insistent upon limiting any activity or planning of NATO to the 'Treaty Area'. This means, of course, that they cannot count upon any assistance from their more powerful colleagues in protecting their own interests further afield — Denmark, for instance, imports eighty per cent of its energy requirements in the form of oil. But that is not a point to which any attention appears to be given in their internal politics, compared with the supposed advantage of reducing to a minimum their own commitments.

The reason why this faith in the Tropic of Cancer turns out to be faith in a myth is an obvious one, though little regard has been given to it. It is that within minutes of the obligations of the Treaty coming into operation as the result of military aggression against the territory of a signatory, the war would be world-wide. The Tropic of Cancer has no meaning to the Soviet Union and the revolutionary allies or satellites which it commands; they are not belligerents confined by any geographical limits, but a global power.

Once they are at war with each of the fifteen Atlantic allies, their submarines, surface craft, aircraft and communist land forces, when they are available, would set about attacking, sinking or capturing their enemies' shipping on every sea, severing their sources of supply and destroying their trade and injuring their nationals. And since NATO has no other *raison d'être* than to prepare for war if it cannot prevent it, there seems to be an unanswerable case for using the whole mechanism of the Alliance to forestall this inevitable consequence of the outbreak of war and make the best disposition to protect its lines of communication, and interests everywhere. Such measures, at which we shall look in a later chapter, would not affect the legal position; no signatories of the Atlantic Treaty could be involved in war unless an attack had been made on the territory, ships or aircraft of any of them in the area specified in the Treaty. It is arguable that, in view of this, it is an abuse of power for a nervous European member government to exploit the rule of unanimity to prevent the North Atlantic Council from taking the precautions which the times demand.

Part Two

Political and Military Developments of the Soviet Union

5 Strategy of the Communist Party

THE DOMINANT POLICY

Since the strategy of the Soviet Union and that of the North Atlantic Alliance are related to one another as cause and effect, it is logical to study first the prevailing posture and probable developments of the former before considering the reaction of the United States and its allies.

It is first necessary to be quite clear on the question where power lies on the Soviet side. Year after year American, British, French and other government spokesmen go on deceiving their public by speaking of the *Russians* as the people with whom they hope to reduce tension or, alternatively, as the authors of operations to which they object, from the military interventions in Hungary, Czechoslovakia, Angola and Afghanistan to the massive rearmament confronting NATO. Yet neither President Brezhnev nor any other leaders or diplomats of the Soviet Union ever describe themselves or their government as Russian. Academics of the Western world have written reams of words on the subject of how far the objectives of the Union of Soviet Socialist Republics are really national and how far ideological, whether the motives for its expanding power are the same as those of the old Empire of the Tsars or whether they are essentially derived from the urge to promote the World Revolution. The majority of soldiers, diplomats and politicians prefer, as did Charles de Gaulle, to treat the phenomenon in terms of the nationalism which they understand rather than in terms of the ideology which they do not; and for the politicians the omission from their speeches of the essential word 'Communist' has the added advantage of not putting up the hackles of the Left and others to whom the Christian Socialism of a former generation has bequeathed a vague sympathy for radical change. It is a foolish and deceptive convention to which the British Foreign Office and Conservative Party are particularly addicted.

43

It is not necessary to engage in this unprofitable debate. It suffices to take three facts as indisputable. The first is that the members of the ruling oligarchy of the Union of Soviet Socialist Republics are all Russians, as are the majority of their subjects; the second is that, whether or not they believe in the idealism of Marx's classless society, they are wholly committed to Communism as a formula for power and the means of winning the class war against Capitalism, an object which admits of no ethical restraints: the third is that their one unquestioned source of authority is the Communist Party of the Soviet Union (CPSU). That and that alone is the government that rules the mass of Russians and the thirty-eight other ethnic groups of which the Union consists; which controls all the armed forces of the Union and of its Warsaw Pact allies; which competes with the United States in strategic nuclear arms; which sees itself as unquestioned head of the "socialist commonwealth", into which, by subversion, political intrigue or military intervention it brings "liberated countries" to join its European satellites as opportunity offers; which operates world-wide mechanisms of propaganda and of espionage; which maintains diplomatic relations of the conventional style with other governments in every camp, and enjoys the right of veto as a Permanent Member of the United Nations Security Council. There is no such centre of power in the Western world.

We shall see later the various organs of the Communist Party, of which the Politburo of the CPSU is the summit, and their relations to the administrative departments of the Union and its component Republics. The First Secretary of the Party, now Leonid Brezhnev, who is also President of the supreme Soviet, is the most powerful figure, as were his predecessors Krushchev and Stalin in their day. It is to the periodical Congresses of the CPSU that we must look for definitions of the overall strategy which, like the Constitution itself, bears the marks of the different phases through which the Soviet Union has passed since the Bolshevik Revolution sixty-three years ago, at the hands of Lenin, its creator, and his successors, phases of which the tyranny of Stalin, the 'Great Patriotic War' and the emergence of the Union as a super-power in the nuclear age are the most significant.

The 'Policy of Peaceful Coexistence', to which I have referred in the first part of this book, is and has been for nearly twenty years the basis of the Soviet Union's main strategy for extending its power in the world without provoking a resort to war by the 'capitalists'. The unprecedented increase in the Union's armaments is mainly, I believe, a means of insurance against the failure of that subtle policy. It also, no doubt, owes a great deal to the strength of the military high command built into the structure of Soviet bureaucracy; to the belief, which Stalin certainly had, that a 'showdown' with the capitalist powers must come, sooner or later; and to the fear of encirclement, inherited from the period between the two world wars and recently revived by the threat of a Chinese — American alliance. The Afghanistan adventure of 1979–80 seems to be a case where the temptation to use military force got out of hand, even though disguised as help to a local revolution. It was a defensive net — but with offensive implications. It certainly caused considerable damage to the Peaceful Coexistence Policy, so far as the United States was concerned, paralysing the SALT II Treaty which had become the show piece of *détente*. What is not easy to understand is how the theorists of Soviet doctrine see the policy of Peaceful Coexistence as a form of struggle between competing social systems — socialism and capitalism — though the advantages which it offers for subversion in non-socialist countries and weakening their will for self-defence has been amply demonstrated. The theory is that time is on the side of the Revolution. During the period of coexistence

the correlation of forces will change, irregularly and possibly with temporary setbacks, but none the less ineluctably, in favour of Communism ... because, according to the doctrine, it follows from the laws of social development and revolution discovered and formulated by Marx, Engels and Lenin. These laws purport to show how pre-communist societies are weakened and eventually destroyed by their own internal contradictions. ... Communists, with their understanding of the underlying laws have the ability and the duty to give history a helping hand when the time becomes ripe for their intervention.[1]

It is difficult to believe that the hard-headed old men of the Politburo in Moscow really take this kind of fatalism seriously, particularly when their industry is so dependent upon the superior technical achievements of capitalist countries; but the whole idiom of the Party, which lacks any of the religious, historical and philosophical background and balance of the European culture, let alone any sense of humour and proportion, has, it must be remembered, a very limited and turgid vocabulary. A simply theory of this kind doubtless suffices to convince the Soviet leaders of their own invincibility. Walter Ulbricht, the late leader of the Socialist Unity Party in East Germany, who was very much in the confidence of his Soviet colleagues said, a few months before the formal adoption of Kruschev's Peaceful Coexistence programme by the CPSU,[2]

> Peaceful Coexistence is a special form of struggle between the forces of socialism and capitalism in the international arena. What we have to do, by clever policies on the part of the Communists and workers' parties and the socialist camp under the leadership of the Soviet Union, is to achieve the maximum results for socialism in this struggle without causing the capitalist opponent to take to arms.

After the 'Great Patriotic War' against Nazi Germany, which the Soviets (with the help of their capitalist allies) eventually won, in spite of the almost irreparable damage which Stalin had done to the Red Army through his insane purge of the best staff officers in 1936 – 8, he set to work with a will to strengthen the Soviet Union's military potential. He acquired as wide a glacis as possible to secure its European frontiers and proceeded to build up a thermo-nuclear armoury, in view of the trial of strength with the United States which he believed to be inevitable. Krushchev, a few years after Stalin's death, observing the swift and formidable reaction of the Americans to the first Soviet sputnik, persuaded the Politburo to give up the idea that victory for the Revolution necessarily required a great military duel with the capitalists. Though never excluding the possibility of it, he had the sense to see the greater probability of mutual thermo-nuclear suicide, and convinced himself that the superiority of the socialist society over the capitalist could overcome the latter by economic means.

> So exhilarated was he by the prospect of the growth in the Soviet economy and technology that in the late 1950s he went so far as to forecast the timetable by which the Soviet Union would overtake the United States. It was an extraordinary proposition. In little more than a decade the Soviet Union was to

become 'first in the world both in total production and in *per capita* production' this century. This country, Krushchev said, 'was moving forward four times as fast as the United States, and the momentum of such progress, reinforced by the surge of Soviet science and technology, came to epitomize for him the basic shift of power between East and West'.[3]

Soviet policy from 1958 to 1962 was greatly influenced by this extraordinary burst of self-confidence; and it was in 1961 that Krushchev won over his colleagues in the Politburo to adopt as its basic strategy the so-called 'Policy of Peaceful Coexistence', which he described as 'an intense form of class struggle in the international arena', a struggle which included the field of politics, economics and ideology but should not take the form of military conflict between states. The policy was written into the official Programme of the CPSU at its XXIInd Congress in October 1961 and has remained part of it to this day, having been endorsed at intervals, particularly in 1971, the year of the Berlin settlement and repeatedly quoted by President Brezhnev.[4] Its purpose is clearly set out in its opening paragraph.

The CPSU considers that the chief aim of its foreign policy activity is to provide peaceful conditions for the building of a Communist society in the USSR and the development of the World Socialist system and, together with other peace-loving peoples to deliver mankind from a war of extermination.

The main thing is to ward off a thermonuclear war, to prevent it breaking out. ...

Peaceful coexistence of the socialist and capitalist countries is an objective necessity for the development of human society.

It is largely a propaganda document containing all the phrases dear to the peace movement of the Western world (e.g. 'non-interference in internal affairs'; 'promotion of economic and cultural cooperation as the basis of complete equality and mutual benefit'), but it identifies peace with the triumph of socialism: 'Imperialism is the only source of the danger of war'. It lists many good intentions, all of which, with the solitary exception of 'the renunciation of war as a means of settling international disputes', that is disputes between sovereign states, have been freely violated by the Soviet Union, either directly or by proxy in the succeeding years, and the contention which I have quoted above[5] that 'Peaceful coexistence facilitates the struggle of the peoples of the colonial and dependent countries for their liberation.'

Krushchev's pre-eminence in the Politburo and his euphoria were soon over. The Cuban Missile Crisis of 1962 showed that he had sadly miscalculated the American spirit. In fact the humiliating return of the missiles under the eyes of the US Navy gave, historically, a great impetus for the development under the inspiration of Admiral Gorshkov of Soviet naval power as we know it today; and one may wonder how far the effective leaders of the Soviet armed forces were ever inclined to put their trust in the formula of peaceful coexistence. Wishful thinking being a characteristic of Western democracy, the ruling politicians of the United States and its allies were beguiled by the apparent evidence of the Soviets' adoption of peaceful methods to advance their cause, to the extent of building upon it, in what seemed to be the mutual interests of both sides, the phantom edifice of *détente*, without realising the danger of the free hand which the CPSU's Peaceful Coexistence policy left it to use the 'liberation' formula to foment and exploit civil war and revolution in any part of the world.

There are thus both strategic gains in the strict military sense, as well as political, economic and technical gains which the CPSU can claim as the result of this important element in its programme during the last nineteen years. I believe that the 'softening up' of the European members of the Atlantic Alliance — the method of Delilah rather than the sling of David — is still the most valuable consequence of it to Moscow. There are times, of course, when the flagrant contradiction between Soviet practice and Soviet propaganda destroys the credibility of the latter, as when the Human Rights 'dissidents' are repressed, or when the military exploitation of a supposed revolutionary situation, as in Afghanistan, gets too near the bone. The Portuguese Revolution was another risky operation which misfired. But President Brezhnev has had more than a formal success, particularly among the Neutrals as well as Russophil elements in the Western Alliance, in internationalising his peaceful coexistence formula at Helsinki.

MILITARY APPLICATION OF THE POLICY

It would be a mistake to consider the actual military strategy of the Soviet Union, meaning the preparation, initiation, conduct and objective of hostilities and the incessant build-up of nuclear power as a subject distinct from the political and ideological, economic and diplomatic objectives defined by the CPSU. Indeed the question when to go to war, is in communist theory primarily determined by the stage which the correlation of forces in the world has reached. One can conceive of a combination of any or all of the following conditions; another and worse energy crisis causing a severe economic depression; the United States, absorbed in controversy between President and Congress, slipping into a state of manifest strategic inferiority; the defensive capacity of the British weakened by persistent industrial disputes and party feuds; Franco–American co-operation in the Atlantic Alliance made precarious by some outburst of anti-American feeling; fear of the Soviet military colossus combined with the attraction of Germany's *Ostpolitik* weakening NATO's defences on the central front; neutralism becoming the dominant political force in Western Europe; growth of a popular anti-nuclear campaign. If in such circumstances the situation seemed auspicious for a 'quick kill', a sudden *blitzkrieg* to overrun Western Europe and destroy the European — American Alliance would be feasible. On the other hand Marshal Sokolovsky in his *Soviet Military Strategy* observes that political progress towards the Communist goal may be so great as to make recourse to war unnecessary.

The XX Congress of the CPSU, on the basis of Marxist—Leninist analysis of the radical changes in the correlation of forces between the two world systems and of the international situation as a whole, concluded that, when the world socialist camp had been converted into a powerful, political, economic and military force and the forces of peace over the entire world have been strengthened, war will not be a fatal inevitability.

There is of course the further consideration that, if, before this blissful state of things is reached, the Soviets were to launch a major war (as distinct from the marginal liberation or revolutionary wars which have not so far involved the West as belligerents) the whole of the psychological and economic gains which their more subtle policies of peaceful coexistence and *détente* had brought them would be lost. It might, of course, be argued that they had served their purpose if victory gave the socialist camp a great extension of territory and population.

A different and, I believe, more cogent reason for the Soviet Union to use its current superiority in nuclear and conventional arms to attack the West in the mid 1980s might be precisely because the correlation of forces is *not* at present developing in the desired direction. After years of reduction in defence budgets in the European NATO countries, after popular reaction in the United States against military commitments overseas and deferment of strategic nuclear arms development because of the hopes of SALT II, quite a substantial process of NATO rearmament is under way. American forces in Europe are on the increase. New and more efficient tanks, aircraft, ships, precision weapons, electronic and anti-submarine warfare devices are being introduced in many of the allied forces. New intermediate-theatre nuclear missiles for Europe are in production. The reintroduction of national service in the United States is projected the new, powerful ICBMs and SLBMs have been commissioned; the British are updating their Polaris missiles with new warheads and plan their replacement with the Trident nuclear submarine and missile system, which would be almost as powerful as the Soviet SLBM, the SS-N-85. But almost all these impressive new additions to the Atlantic armoury are only due to be deployed or to become operational *four, five, six or ten years ahead*. It is true that the Soviet arms industry is pouring out land, sea and air armaments and nuclear novelties even faster. But the temptation to strike before the ten-year rearmament of NATO reaches its intended term must be considerable.

We cannot possibly tell whether, when or where an offensive by the Soviet forces might begin, whether on the Central German Front on which the bulk of the Soviet armour is massed; as General Hackett and his collaborators guess in their *The Third World War*;[6] in the extreme North, weakly defended, where a great naval force could debouch into the Northern Atlantic; or in one or more drives outside the Atlantic Treaty area. Of these an attempted conquest of the oil-rich Arabian Gulf area is the preferred speculation of many American military commentators.

An operation outside the treaty area, which compelled the United States to fight, would have the initial advantage of separating them from their European allies, who would be under no legal obligation to intervene, a point to which insufficient attention has been given. The Soviet forces, however, would have difficulty in getting to grips with their principal antagonist without violating the land, territorial waters and airspace of his European allies, if only because of the need of access to the oceans. Reviewing the well-known series of articles on *Navies in Peace and War* by Admiral Gorchkov in the naval review. *Morskoi Sbernik*, an English naval author writes:

> He lays considerable stress on Russia's natural handicaps and the need to overcome them in order to gain unhindered access to the oceans and the seas. He places great emphasis on gaining control of the Bosphorus and the Dardanelles and clearly does not rule out the possibility of a limited war in order to gain this long-sought objective.[7]

The control of the narrow passage between Denmark and Sweden would be no less essential for the Baltic Fleet to break out. These considerations alone would involve aggression against Turkey and Denmark, which would bring the Atlantic Treaty into operation, as would an attack upon any other member of the Alliance, such as Italy through intervention in Yugoslavia. The probability is that any major military initiative by the Soviet Union would be in the context of the Warsaw Pact and almost inevitably involve NATO as a whole. It is the considered judgment of General Hackett and his fellow speculators that France, though outside the NATO framework, would be true to her treaty obligations and fight.

Apart from these speculations, however, there are certain characteristics of Soviet strategic planning which we should mention. The first is the absolute co-ordination of the armed forces' activities, not only with the general theories of Marxist — Leninism but with the current political operations of the Soviet state. Lord Carrington, in answer to proposals for military action to counter the moves of the Soviet in the area of the Gulf in January 1980, insisted that subversion was the primary danger to meet. It is indeed true that, in every war in which the Soviets have intervened outside Europe, military action has been preceded or accompanied by some form of civil conflict or rebellion. In Europe circumstances do not lend themselves to these methods and it is difficult to find peoples who require to be liberated from imperialist oppression. But it would be reasonable to look for the exacerbation of social, industrial or political conflicts wherever possible and propaganda designed to weaken national resistance. The Soviet Union has the advantage of an in-built fifth column in most European Countries.

A second point is the insistence in all Soviet military manuals on the importance of instant attack. The Soviets are not inhibited by any of the popular doubts, controversies and constitutional complexities, television and press reporting which characterise the democratic countries. This greatly facilitates a sudden offensive. Certainly the order of battle of the Warsaw Pact troops on the Central Front envisages sudden attack without warning from a standing start, probably by means of a number of swift spear-head thrusts by joint forces of tanks and BMPS with maximum air and artillery cover. Soviet strategy is geared to pre-emption: that is to attack first given the inevitability of a NATO offensive. The 'trigger' could be an actual decision to mobilise in some future crisis.

How far does Soviet strategic planning involve the use of nuclear arms? It is very possible that for political reasons as well as to avoid the danger of provoking a strategic nuclear response, the Soviet Union would not be the first to use nuclear weapons; but it has always been assumed that a major show-down with the capitalists would become a nuclear war, and all the Warsaw Pact forces are prepared for it. The avoidance of thermo-nuclear war is, as we have seen, the first official aim of the Policy of Peaceful Coexistence but, though the Soviet Government is a party to various international agreements for limiting nuclear power, the Red Army is more thoroughly prepared than any other national forces both for the use of nuclear arms and for protection against nuclear radiation; and the same applies, both actively and passively, to chemical warfare.

As regards the strategic intercontinental missiles, it is said that the Soviet High Command accepts the official policy of numerical equivalence with the United States as embodied in the SALT II Treaty but there is no pause in the technical development of their accuracy, throw-weight, and capacity and in the production of new models. There is no check upon the construction and deployment of the intermediate-range missiles, of which the SS20 is the most formidable. The prospects of bringing them and the new United States' theatre nuclear arms, intended to counteract them, within the scope of treaty limitation are very doubtful especially since SALT II has not been ratified. But there are two aspects of general nuclear strategy which are important. In the first place, none of the distinctions which the Americans, and consequently NATO, make between the different grades of nuclear warfare, tactical, intermediate and intercontinental (strategic) and of escalation between them, or ideas of graduated, flexible response, have any place in Soviet military thinking. Obviously the logical rule that no more force is used than is necessary for victory, local or otherwise, would apply as in all military or police operations. But the Soviet view is that whatever seems necessary for success at any stage *will* be used, taking account, no doubt, of the enemy's power of response; and this applies to nuclear and chemical arms as well as any others.

The other point which distinguishes Soviet strategic thinking from that of the West is that it does not accept the notion that there can be no winner in a nuclear war. Thus the American-made notion of 'mutual assured destruction' means nothing to the Soviets, nor does 'deterrence'. They are convinced that a nuclear war could be fought and won, whatever the cost. Their own ICBMs are designed for attacks, as precise as possible, upon the enemy's strategic missiles in their silos, military bases, government and command centres, rather than for the annihilation of cities. They would certainly not hesitate to use MIRVed missiles for terror purposes if policy so required, and it is particularly the intermediate missiles designed for European targets which seem to have this character. The evidence of their belief in their ability to survive nuclear attack is the number of massive shelters which they have built for the members of the Politburo and the rest of the Party hierarchy in the first place, then for administrative and military headquarters, then for as many as possible of the population employed in key industries. The whole attitude of the CPSU to conventional and nuclear military power is summed up in the following conclusion of three well-qualified American experts:

Soviet leaders are determined to amass military power for the purpose of bringing about an increasingly favourable 'cor-

relation of world forces' in order to accelerate the world revolutionary purpose and erode the Western position. They
believe that the United States, the world's principal 'status quo'
and counterrevolutionary power is being compelled to reconcile itself to the realities of Soviet power rather than risk its
own destruction.[8]

The theory that the Soviet is the centre of a world-wide
Socialist Commonwealth is reflected in the relation between the
forces of the Soviet Union itself and those of its satellite and allied
states. The former are united under Soviet Command in the
Warsaw Pact, and of these a certain number of East Germans
and Czechs are used as 'advisers' in African ventures. The forces
of the allies, Cubans, Vietnamese, and Ethiopians are under the
orders of their own governments, though the Soviet Union equips
and pays for any common operation. How reliable these satellites
and surrogate forces would be in a world war is anyone's guess. In
the third edition of Marshal Sokolevsky's *Soviet Military Strategy*
we read; 'The USSR will render, when it is necessary, military
support as such to people subject to imperialist aggression.'
Southern Africa seems to be the only area which still qualifies for
this beneficent attention. Now that the victims of colonialism
have nearly run out of stock, one wonders on whom the blessings
of liberation will be bestowed. But where there's a will there's a
way.

6 Some internal characteristics and problems

Seen from without, the aspects of that great Socialist experiment, started by the Russian Revolution sixty-three years ago, which absorb the interest of foreign observers, are chiefly its external effects. It is consequently, with its strategy of political expansion, its capacity for attaining its avowed ends by military or other means and the reactions, whether of resistance or accommodation, that this phenomenon provokes, that this book is concerned. But, while it is perfectly legitimate to study the internal affairs of the Soviet Union and its allies or satellites, as well as their economic and financial relations with the rest of the world from the same standpoint, we are, I am sure, likely to have quite an inaccurate picture if we try to apply the criteria of Western democracy to the political and social conditions and outlook of the Soviet peoples.

There are indeed important distinctions to be drawn between the Soviet Union and each of the six very different neighbours subject to its control; but of all of them it is true that the Communist Party is the ruling class which holds all the levers of power and positions of influence at every level. In the Soviet Union itself it is the Establishment, in much the same way as the gentry, the middle class, the professions and the Church of England were the Establishment of Victorian England. It is an elite of 16 million out of a total population of about 260 million; the proportion of the population in the other Socialist countries — the German Democratic Republic, Poland, Czechoslovakia, Hungary, Romania — is smaller, having been formed around a political nucleus imposed from without.

And what of the 244 million people in the Soviet Union who are not Party members? In the view of Sir Fitzroy Maclean, who has had the unusual advantage of travelling freely through different parts of the country with which he has long been familiar:

> it is a reasonable assumption that, human nature being what it is, they take neither more nor less interest in politics than do the mass of people in other countries. What primarily concerns them are their families, their jobs, their homes, their ways of life and standards of living. In all these respects they will have noticed, especially if they are over 40, a marked improvement over the years.[1]

One of the most evil things the Communist leaders have done is to build and maintain by their propaganda a barrier of spurious political hatred between the Russian people and the rest of us, whom they constantly describe as bloodthirsty warmongers, imperialists, capitalists, oppressors, etc. In fact, apart from an occasional Party-sponsored demonstration against a Moscow Embassy, one hears of no sign of personal ill-felling among the citizens of Moscow or any other parts of that vast country against foreigners, American or European.

Thanks to the greater opportunities of information and entertainment which cannot be stifled and the aid of the 'parallel market', many of the external characteristics of Western society are being avidly copied and adopted, and some recent improvements in housing, shopping and living conditions encourage the process. It is, perhaps, the least admirable clothes and crazes of foreign youth, and American stunts of the moment which attract the Russian teenager, but, for what these manifestations (or at a rather higher level, imitations of Paris fashions) are worth, they certainly exhibit the reverse of any antipathy to the West. I have no doubt that, if there were real freedom of contact between the Russians and the peoples of Western Europe and North America, there would be a wealth of exchange in every variety of human life, cultural, spiritual, sporting, artistic, urban and rural, serious and humorous, which would be an immense mutual enrichment. I interject this thought as a safeguard against the lamentable habit of assuming that 'The Russians' whom we are obliged to oppose, are really 'The Russians', and not their all-powerful ruler, the Communist Party of the Soviet Union.

PARTY AND PEOPLE

All powerful it evidently is, not only in its grip upon the whole machinery of government, by controlling and duplicating every Ministry and department of the Union and its component Republics and ensuring that only its nominees are chosen, by the solemn caricature of democracy which is observed in the periodical elections of the Supreme Soviet, its Praesidium and other lesser bodies at the different levels. The power of the secret police remains, with the sinister penal apparatus of banishment, prison, forced labour, or the psychiatric hospital in the background, to discourage any sign of non-conformity. Marxism — Leninism has been drummed into everyone at school and in the forces and censorship, though slightly loosened of late, has succeeded for three generations in insulating most people from the movement of ideas in the rest of the world. It is the most effective totalitarian government which history has known.

How long can it last? Human nature is the worst enemy of arbitrary political systems. It may gradually have a dissolvent effect, just as the fruit, vegetables, eggs and meat from the small private plots of the peasantry, erstwhile only grudgingly permitted in contrast to collectivism, have come to account for thirty per cent of the fresh food on sale: and the 'parallel market' for household goods and repairs, clothes, automobile spare parts and maintenance, has become almost a recognised institution. Whether the cases of bribery and corruption of which one reads are any worse than in non-socialist countries it is hard to tell: they are the inevitable consequence of a regimented economy. It is undeniable that, by a natural evolution, a distinctive class system has developed, based not indeed upon land and heredity, but upon status and its material awards. Thus we hear of a middle class, so long lacking in Russia, emerging in the life of the towns as against the privileged upper crust of high Party officials, service chiefs and their families.

The official anti-religious policy undoubtedly goes against the grain of millions particularly in the villages, as we shall see; and the standing affront of Russian Communist control to the indestructible patriotisms of the troops of the Warsaw Pact allies poses a lasting question mark over their reliability in case of war. I am inclined also to believe that the aversion to war of the bulk of the Soviet population, which is likely to increase as life becomes more worth living, is a greater deterrent to a decision to risk a nuclear war than the Communist braggodocio of inevitable victory for the cause of Socialism would lead us to believe.

But these are only speculations. What is undeniable is the hold which the Party has on the country, not only because of its powerful mechanism but because of the relative success, despite much bureaucratic inefficiency, of its planned economy and the extent to which, under its rule, the lot of so large a part of the working population has been gradually bettered. Jerry F. Hough and Merle Fainsod, looking to the future in the concluding chapter of their thorough and balanced account, *How the Soviet Union is Governed*,[2] write:

> While collectivisation and repression eroded many early sources of support, the Party did come to be associated with a highly successful industrialization program and especially with restoration of the nation's position in the international area and with the achievement of historic national goals.
>
> After victory in World War II the Party also became associated with a steadily rising standard of living and an apparent solution to the problems of unemployment and inflation which came to plague Western economies in these years. Probably most important of all, rule by the Communist Party was accompanied by upward mobility for a large percentage of the Soviet people.[3]

'Is my job of higher status than that of my father?' That is what 'upward mobility' means to a large number of Soviet citizens as Table 6.1 shows. If they are accurate, which I have no reason to doubt, they can only be explained by an extraordinary expansion of University education and technical training.

TABLE 6.1

	1959	1970
Higher education, white collar workers	6 115 000	14 790 000
Lower education, white collar workers	10 650 000	16 030 000
Skilled labour (excluding light industry)	18 330 000	29 860 000
Skilled labour (in light industry)	2 900 000	3 625 000
Higher skilled labour in agriculture	3 500 000	3 925 000
Unskilled labour in agriculture	30 365 000	18 680 000

As for advancement in the administrative sphere, Mr Brezhnev claimed in a speech made in 1971, that:

> Over 80% of the present secretaries of republican central committees and *oblast* and *kray* party committees, and the Chairmen of the republican Council of Ministers and executive committees of the *kray* and *oblast* Soviets, began their activity as workers and peasants, as did around 70% of the U.S.S.R. Ministers and Chairmen of State Committees.

Improvement in pay and status is very closely linked with membership of the Party. Membership is, of course, a condition of office in the state, republican and local Soviets, and there are said to be high levels of membership among the more technical, middle ranks of administrative personnel. But not everyone is encouraged to apply for acceptance as a candidate. For membership, whether in a high or low position, whether in the army or civilian life, in the large or small Primary Party Organisation which exists in every factory or business, requires active work for the Party. This includes (in theory at least) the promotion of Communist doctrine and propaganda, contributing to the productivity of the enterprise and exposing any bureaucratic obstruction. Thus it involves a sense of responsibility as part of the establishment. The Party has, in fact, become more middle-aged in its membership with the passing of time. Thus on 1 January 1978, 5.8 per cent only of the members and candidates were 25 years of age or under, 10.8 per cent were from 26-30 years old, 25.9 per cent were 31-40, 26 per cent were 41-50, 18.1 per cent were 51-60, and 13 per cent were over 60 years of age.[4]

NO SIGN OF POLITICAL CHANGE

These figures give an idea of how deeply the Party is integrated in the organisation and management of the life of society in almost all its aspects, military and civilian, administrative, industrial and agricultural, educational, scientific and cultural. Apart from resentment at the Party's hostility to religion, which comes to the surface on occasion, there does not seem to be tension between the population as a whole and the Party which is accepted as 'the powers that be'. Where friction exists it is in the periphery, the recently annexed areas of the Baltic Republics the former Polish Ukraine and Moldavia, and in the adjoining satellite states, Poland and Czechoslovakia in particular. The task of holding together in a single political, economic and legal system six or seven nations, each with its own history and customs, as the Russian Communists have attempted to do since the end of the Second World War, in addition to the ethnic divisions within the Soviet Union itself, can only be achieved by superior force. If a system of constitutional democracy with free elections were allowed to evolve in Eastern Europe, nothing is more certain than that an anti-Russian party would sweep the board, and this would very likely find an echo in the non-Russian borderlands of the Soviet Union. This is a cogent reason for resisting any movement towards democracy in the Soviet Union itself and it explains why the government is so disturbed by, and so ruthless in its suppression of the small number of intellectual dissidents and defenders of 'Human Rights', who are hardly known to the Russian public outside Moscow and Lithuania. Yet there is no denying that a Solzhenitzyn or a Sakharov is a very genuine Russian, and there must be many others who in their heart of hearts share, as Russians, the moral and humane standards of the Christian civilisation; but why should the ordinary citizen and family man ask for trouble?

As Sir Fitzroy Maclean writes:

> The average Russian is still very much aware of the KGB and, unless he himself happens to have a connection with it, anxious to keep out of its way. He will also be extremely conscious of the Party hierarchy and, in particular, of the Party secretary or organiser at the place of work where he lives. He is well aware that any openly subversive activity on his part would immediately be reported to the 'competent authorities' and that he would be in trouble. If on the other hand a man keeps quiet and does a good job of work, he should have nothing to worry about.[5]

SOME ECONOMIC AND POLITICAL CONSTRAINTS

Are there any weaknesses of the Soviet regime today which have a bearing upon its external relations? There is a kind of ritual enumeration of these supposed weaknesses, put forward (in 1979–80) by official American spokesmen as an antidote to the Soviets' undoubted increase of military power. We find it in Henry Kissinger's well-known discourse on the future of NATO at Brussels in September 1979, in which, after noting the low figure of the GNP of the Soviet Union compared to that of the United States, he went on to say 'the Soviet Union has leadership problems, social problems and minority problems'. The same line of argument was repeated by General Rogers. Except for the obvious difficulties, which have not changed substantially in a quarter of a century of holding together in the Warsaw Pact and Comecon an international amalgam of peoples and of containing their potentially anti-Communist nationalism, to which I have referred, I find little evidence to substantiate these suggestions in the Soviet Union itself. 'Leadership problems' are indeed the stock-in-trade of the periodical American Presidential elections; it is too early to judge whether any comparable rivalries will follow the eventual eclipse of President Brezhnev. Of disruptive minority problems, such as those with which the United Kingdom, or Spain, or Belgium or Canada are only too familiar, there is at present no sign. The growing proportion of Muslims in the forces may indeed create a serious problem for the CPSU in the future, in view of the current Islamic resurgence; for the Muslims are certainly less Sovietised and subject to less anti-religious harassment than the Orthodox or Ex-Orthodox and other Christian populations, Muslim soldiery engaged in the early stages of the invasion of Afghanistan are said to have been replaced when they were picking up as many copies of the Koran as they could. But this is not yet a major issue.

In his speech at the last Party Congress, President Brezhnev complained of the disappointing performance of the economy and was particularly critical of the failure of the chemical industry to fulfil expectations, a grievance reflected in the slogans issued for May Day 1980. There were criticisms also of the efficiency of the building industry and of the pace of construction of the new Baikal — Amur Main railway line, upon which so much of the exploitation of Eastern Siberian resources depends.

It is difficult to see how such deficiencies of the Planned Economy — compared, for example, with the United States' failure to solve its energy problem or the *hara-kiri* of the British Motor industry — have any bearing upon the external strength or weakness of the Soviet Union. A more tell-tale May Day slogan may, indeed, reflect the stoppage of American grain for animal feed and at the same time the Party's dissatisfaction at the poor yield of state, as against private, production. 'Toilers in agriculture! Strengthen the fodder basis of animal husbandry! Raise the production and sale to the state of meat, milk, eggs, wool and other products.'

Apart from such matters of detail, experts point to three constraints upon the Government. One is the perennial inadequacy of hard currency and the consequent need for foreign credits; another is the manpower shortage; another, the growing demand of the public for better goods to buy.

THE NEED FOR HARD CURRENCY

The economy is basically sound.

> The U.S.S.R. is the only major industrial nation in the world that is self-sufficient in energy and likely to maintain this position in the foreseeable future. Oil sales to the West are the Soviet Union's largest single source of hard currency earnings, totalling some thirty-two billion dollars in 1975.[6]

There are also large coal exports to the West, and the Soviet Union is building up a sizeable export in natural gas. Energy supply, according to the latest Ten Year Plan, should grow at an annual rate of five per cent, but for this, since the wells in the Ural — Volga area are becoming exhausted, it is necessary to exploit the great Siberian deposits of petroleum and gas. It is in this frozen world that expensive Western and Japanese technology and equipment are particularly needed, such as thousands of miles of oil pipe line. At present eighty per cent of the energy used in the Soviet Union is consumed in the western part of the country whereas eighty per cent of the resources are east of the Urals.[7] Hence the demand for foreign credits to supplement the hard currency obtained by the Soviet Union's own exports and from the import — export banks of its Comecon allies. This is the sensitive area where foreign and defence policies impinge upon economic interest. The chief value of the Helsinki Conference operation to Moscow was, of course, the stimulus which it gave to the acquisition of technical 'know-how' and inventions from the West and to government and bank credits to finance the contracts involved. The foreign debts of the Soviet Union itself (in 1977) came to $12 thousand million and those of Comecon as a whole to $48 thousand million. Any political or military action which seriously affronts the United States and other Western creditors, as did the Afghanistan escapade, can jeopardise these transactions, apart from the denial of Western technology on defence grounds for which the COCOM system provides.

Expert opinion differs widely on the actual value of imported inventions to the industrial production of the Soviet Union. The frustrating delays of Soviet factories, clogged by the rules of the planned economy in following up foreign technical processes, are notorious. On the other hand one can point to the practical consequences of certain imports (e.g. fertilisers; passenger-car production) which have been outstandingly successful.

MANPOWER SHORTAGE

Shortage of manpower is already being felt in certain industries. It will become serious in the next few years because it is estimated that the growth rate of the population at the end of the century will have dropped to about a third of what is was in the 1950s. This will mean a much slower rate of growth in the labour force. The implications of this for the heavy industries and especially those employed in the ceaseless production of military weapons and vehicles are serious. For this reason as well as on financial grounds, some American experts believe that there will be considerable pressure to reduce defence expenditure or at least limit it to an increase of only two or three per cent a year instead of the present rate which is double that figure. It is the Russian birthrate which is falling, unlike that of the Central Asian Republics: the Muslims are already a third of the population of the Soviet Union and are on the increase.

DEMAND FOR CONSUMER GOODS

The demand for better and more varied food, clothes and accompaniments of civilised living, especially in Moscow and other cities, is something which the ruling oligarchy can no longer ignore. Whether it is the result of observing foreign visitors and the special shops provided for them or what one sees on television or buys in Prague or Warsaw or Budapest, it is borne in upon Russian townsmen and women that, though they may be earning more, conditions of life are lower than they are in other countries. Only four per cent of the people, for instance, have cars: they have to wait for months to get one and more often than not must rely on the black market to have it delivered or serviced. Communist propaganda is no answer to the resulting discontent. There are, of course, prosperous country areas in the warm south of European Russia and the Caucasus, but they are the exception. It is evident that the successors to the Brezhnev era will have to devote a much larger proportion of their budget to consumer goods. Thirty per cent of the population is still employed in agriculture, the productivity of which, as a whole, is far below that of Western Europe or North America. Hence the chronic dependence upon imported grain, especially for cattle food (and therefore the supply of meat) to compensate for the vagaries of the weather and the harvest, culminating in the eight-year contract with the United States, which, of course, means a great deal to the farmers of the Middle West in that country. President Carter's withholding of eighteen million tons of grain in 1980, in protest at the Afghanistan invasion, was therefore, a serious matter.

THE PRICE OF ATHEISM

It is worth looking a little more closely at the anti-religious commitment of the Communist Government to which I have alluded, for it is part of an endless duel against nature which is liable in the long run to be a serious source of weakness to the Socialist cause. Denial of the existence of God is a basic tenet of Marxist—Leninism and, though for reasons of expediency the right to practice, though not to propagate religious belief is allowed in the Soviet constitution, its exercise is so hedged around with restrictions that it is easy, whenever opportunity offers, for authority to make it inoperative. There have been times when the anti-God campaign has been pursued with great vigour and brutality; this gave the Russian Orthodox Church many martyrs in the early years of the Revolution. There are still periodical outbursts of this, notably in the *Komsomol*; but the necessity of recognising the rooted religious tradition of the Russian people when appealing to their patriotism in the Second World War has had its effect upon the Politburo since then. The territorial consequences of victory thereupon brought millions of other Christians, mainly Catholics, within the power of the CPSU, both within the frontiers of the Soviet Union and in the adjoining states overrun by the Red Army. This made it necessary for the Communists, in the interest of foreign policy, to adopt more subtle and varied ways of dealing with the Churches.

The most recent stage of the resulting battle of wits has been the partial success of the *Ostpolitik* of the Holy See, initiated by Pope Paul VI and continued by his Polish successor, John Paul II, in re-establishing the hierarchy in Hungary with bishops acceptable to the Communist Government. In Poland, where nine-tenths of the nation are practising Catholics, Cardinal Wyszynski and his fellow bishops proved too strong for such political control, and the anti-religious regime is restricted to administrative obstruction. The immense popularity of the Pope's visit in 1979, not only in Poland itself but throughout Eastern Europe, was an epoch-making rebuff to the atheism of the Communist rulers.

In Russia itself, since Stalin's day, the CPSU has tended to revert to the Tsarist policy of patronising and using the hierarchy of the Russian Orthodox Church as an instrument of government, while taking every opportunity, on one pretext or another, to reduce the number of churches available for worship and to discourage any spiritual activity outside the limits of liturgical ceremony. This policy has enabled the Soviet Government to employ the Patriarch of Moscow and his higher clergy, who are now in effect Communist agents, for the advancement of their own propaganda in the international ecumenical meetings which are now the order of the day, notably in the World Council of Churches. The government has also exploited the nationalism of the Orthodox Church by compelling some two million Uniate Catholics of the annexed Polish Ukraine to conform to it. All their Bishops were arrested and have died in prison, except Archbishop Slipyi, who was eventually released and exiled in 1964. The Lithuanians, an almost entirely Catholic people, have been subjected to constant hostile pressure, every effort being made to intimidate their clergy and seminarists and to dictate the appointment of Bishops and pastors. Laymen and women endeavouring to teach the faith to children have been sentenced to long terms of imprisonment.

There has been evidence lately of serious resentment among Orthodox believers of whom, it is claimed, there are thirty million in the Soviet Union, both of the intermittent ill-treatment of country parishes and of the Patriarch's fawning upon the government. An example of the former is worth citing. It was the decision of the authorities to requisition the Orthodox Church in Zanosy, a large Ukrainian village, for grain storage. This led to a general strike, the men refusing to go back to work on the collective farm and the children to go to school. The district authorities thereupon deported the inhabitants to another village 'allegedly for work with the ducks'. Then, according to the report:

> Five busloads of militia and two lorries arrived at the church. Hooking hawsers to the building they began to tear it apart in all directions. The deceived parishioners returned wailing to Zanosy and, surrounding the church, demanded an end to the satanic work. The militia mercilessly twisted the arms of men and women. ... In the morning the local authorities, under the command of the procurator of Sarny District, burnt down the church. The charred remains of the church smouldered and the people wept.

This was not the end of the story:

> People began to come from all the surrounding villages to Zanosy. They prayed and hung ornaments on the pine trees near the ashes of the church. The authorities' efforts to stop them, including sealing the village, were useless. They decided to cut down the pines.[8]

The flattery of the Soviet Government by the Orthodox Hierarchy and the criticism which it evokes are revealed in the following incident, which seems to have been widely known in Moscow. Father Gleb Yakunin wrote to the Patriarch Pimen on behalf of the Christian Committee for the Defence of Believers' Rights in the USSR, objecting to his letter to President Brezhnev printed in the *Journal of the Moscow Patriarchate* (No. 2,1979), in which he wrote: 'Your radiant image, your high humanitarian ideals and your personal charm leave an unforgettable impression on all those who are fortunate enough to come into contact with you.' It is hardly surprising that Father Yakunin as well as Father Dmitri Dudko, the pastor of a suburban Moscow parish, whose sermons had been attracting large congregations, including young people, were put on trial in March 1980. The opening of the trials was the occasion for an outburst of official denunciation, reported in *Pravda*, against all manner of active Christian, Orthodox, unregistered Baptists, Jehovah's Witnesses, Lithuanian Catholics. It was difficult to tell whether this was the beginning of a prolonged punitive operation or only a temporary outburst. What is extraordinary is the apparently erratic vacillations of official policy. For these public denunciations — possibly a sop thrown to the Anti-God militants of the Party — followed an exceptional event, the visit, at the invitation of Patriarch Pimen, of Cardinal Lékai, the Hungarian Catholic Primate, who was allowed in October 1979 to celebrate Mass in the Lithuanian Republic at Kaunas and Vilnius, attended by vast crowds. It was no doubt a way of cashing in, for political purposes, on the Vatican's *Ostpolitik*. But there can be no doubt that the reaction both in the Soviet Union itself and, even more, in all the Warsaw Pact countries, to the official hostility to the people's religion is a more serious cause of weakness to the rule of the CPSU than is commonly realised.

7 The military organisation of the Soviet Union

Before describing the actual military forces of the Soviet Union and their armaments, it is well to have as accurate a picture as possible of the system which produces, develops and maintains them. And here, as in so many other aspects of the comparison between Western countries and the Soviet Union, we must begin by realising a radical difference in the whole conception of defence. In the United Kingdom's annual budget, for instance, defence is an item which comes some way down the list of public expenditure, after pensions and allowances, national health, social services and education. It is the poor relation of Labour Governments but enjoys a revival of interest under a Conservative Government. In the United States, owing to the cost of the nuclear establishment and the very high pay of servicemen, the Federal Defence Budget is large, but it is still only a small part of the public expenditure of the Federation and the States as a whole. The situation differs in western European countries, but in none of them is defence the main cost which the national revenue has to bear. Nor is this surprising for people who look upon peace and stability as normal, and preparation for war as abnormal and regrettable.

For the Soviet Union, however, military power is the necessary instrument of its national and ideological purpose, not only as its contribution to the changing correlation of forces in the world which are destined to culminate in the victory of Socialism, but to defend that process against the hostile capitalists. Defence, there-fore, penetrates the whole fabric of society; and, even if Marxism — Leninism, despite the incessant indoctrination, is no more than a mental habit for many people, the basic patriotism of the Russians is a firm foundation upon which the Party can build the universal obligation of defence. Politicians of the Atlantic Alliance find great difficulty in adding the agreed three per cent increase to their defence budgets. Even under a Conservative Government the three per cent target has not been reached in the United Kingdom in either of the two financial years 1979 — 80, 1981 — 2. But there seems to be no internal objection in the Soviet Union to the government spending twelve or thirteen per cent of its GNP for military purposes, a proportion that, some experts believe, is likely to rise to twenty per cent in the 1980s. It is only the demographic factor, resulting from a falling birthrate, which is beginning to slow down the rate of expansion on defence.

MILITARY SERVICE

To start at the bottom of the pyramid of military organisation in the Soviet Union, every boy — and this applies as much to the Central Asian Republics as to the Russian and European Republics — is educated for military service. Pre-military — and political — training starts at school. At the age of ten boys and girls join the Pioneers. At fourteen a boy may join the Komsomol, the league of Young Communists, active membership of which ends at twenty-eight. The Law of Universal Military Service of 1967 provides for introductory military training for all youths, whether in schools, farms, or other enterprises and institutions for two years before they are liable for active service at the age of eighteen. Service in the army and air force is for two years, and in the navy, border troops and certain special forces for three. It is not clear whether the recruit has any choice between services, but it seems that the navy has an appeal for a good number and it is said that naval fathers, especially if they are officers, are apt to secure naval service for their sons. Only about half the annual cohort of eighteen-year-olds (about 1.3 million) is actually called up, including those picked for officer training in special establishments. The remainder are liable to be drafted at any time. Periodical refresher courses for them, and, at less frequent intervals, for those who have completed their regular service and pass (until they are fifty) into the Reserve, are sponsored by the 'All Union Voluntary Society for Assistance to the Army, the Air Force and the Navy', DOSAAF, which also organises the pre-service training, using professional military instructors. A valuable addition to the conscript forces is the 'extended military service' of volunteers, open to soldiers, sailors and particularly sergeants and master-sergeants about to be discharged into the

Reserve, as well as well-qualified servicemen already in the Reserve who are not over thirty-five.

These volunteers, who may enlist for two, four or six years, are evidently of importance for specialised duties in the air force and army and administration. They probably number about 400 000.

The proportion of officers to non-commissioned personnel is very high.[1] In the army, in contrast to the ageing higher command who are still mainly Second World War veterans, sixty-five per cent of the regimental officers are under thirty.[2]

The present strength of the six Soviet armed services (according to the International Institute for Strategic Studies (IISS), *The Military Balance 1979—80*)is as follows: Strategic Rocket Forces 375 000: Air Defence (PVO Strany) 550 000; Internal Security Troops (Ministry of the Interior) 500 000; Army 1 825 000; Navy 433 000; Air Force 475 000; total 4 158 000.

From the Reserve the Category II and Category III Divisions of the army can very quickly be made up to strength, when necessary. The fact that Divisions stationed in the greater part of Soviet territory are only manned up to half-strength or quarter strength, while those in the Group of Soviet Forces in Germany, for instance (Category I), are fully manned and equipped, allows for a large number of young Reservists at any given time to be used in industry.

THE MILITARY DISTRICTS

The Soviet Union is divided into sixteen Military Districts, a system which the Communists took over from Tsarist Russia (the Odessa Military District dates from 1862), but have adapted, taking account of the lessons of the 'Great Patriotic War' and the requirements of the nuclear age. The Districts vary greatly in the strength of their army and air formations. The most powerful are Belorussian (HQ Minsk); Leningrad; Baltic (HQ Riga); Carpathian (HQ Lvov); Moscow; Kiev; Odessa; Trans-Baikal (HQ Chita), and the Far Eastern (HQ Khabarovsk).

Military Education is one of the standing responsibilities of the Military District Commander, under the control of the Main Political Administration, which is the principal organ of the Party—Military Structure. All troops within the Soviet Union, except the Strategic Rocket Forces — the élite of the army — and the National Air Defence, are under the orders of the Military District Commanders and so are the frontal aviation squadrons. The Commanders are also responsible for mobilisation and have the duty of coping with civil disorder, for which their troops would co-operate with those of the KGB and MVD. Communist Party officials are prominent in the headquarters staff of every District. The Military Council of the District includes, in addition to the Service Chiefs, the First Secretary of the Party in the local Republic or *oblast*. Alongside of the command structure is the Military Commisariat, the *Voenkomat*, represented at every level, which is responsible for the supply of military manpower, including the call-up of reservists and also the temporary use of the soldiery for construction or other necessary civilian work. At the national level the *Voenkomat*, of which there are 3700 branches, comes under the control of the 3rd (Mobilisation) Directorate of the Soviet General Staff. In theory each District is, in all that pertains to order and security, a state in miniature, an independent theatre of operations 'capable of fighting without external direction in the event of nuclear war'.[3] This theory could only really apply to the larger Military Districts. Several are in fact combined for strategic purposes in 'theatres of military operations' (TVD). According to Professor Erickson.[4]

> Obviously, a Military District could not sustain wartime operations in isolation, whatever its peacetime role in maintaining particular forces in being and mobilisation apparatus. Perhaps a clue is provided by the organisation of the Operations Directorate of the Soviet General Staff which is divided into six 'operational branches', the Northern, the Western, the Balkans, the Near East, Central Asia and the Far East.

In addition to the military map of the Soviet Union itself, there are four 'Groups of Forces' in the neighbouring Socialist countries of the Warsaw Pact, the Group of Soviet Forces in the German Democratic Republic (350 000 men); the Central Group in Czechoslovakia (55 000 — 60 000); the Northern Group in Poland (32 000 — 35 000) and the Southern Group in Hungary (40 000 — 50 000). The armies, air forces, and, in the case of the GDR, Poland, Romania and Bulgaria, navies, of the members of the Warsaw Pact also, of course, come under the Soviet High Command, and for this there is a special staff. The TVDs, in which the Military Districts bordering the Soviet frontiers are involved as well as the Groups of Forces outside them, include participation in military operations (in the event of war) in the NATO area to the West and South, China, Korea and Japan in the East.

For the navy, a series 'Ocean Theatres of Operation' (OTVDs) is defined. These are divided between the four Fleet Commands, Northern, Baltic, Black Sea and Pacific. There is not as yet a separate Indian Ocean Command.

NUCLEAR WEAPONS

How does the great array of Soviet nuclear missiles fit into this overall plan? The submarine-launched ballistic missiles and any ship-borne tactical nuclear weapons are clearly a naval command responsibility subject to general policy decisions. On land the strategic and intermediate nuclear missile systems are not territorially deployed in the Military Districts organisation. The Strategic Rocket Forces (350 000 strong) who operate all of them (e.g. SS20s as well as ICBMs) are under the direct command of the Deputy Defence Minister concerned. In fact their deployment is dictated by geography and targeting requirements (European, Chinese or intercontinental); and the ABM system, now much reduced surrounds Moscow. 'The Air Defence System is organised into two major Air Defence Districts, Moscow and Baku, whose early warning radars reach out far to the north west and south west respectively.'[5]

THE CENTRAL MECHANISM

The central mechanism for the direction of the Soviet Union's military activity is far more complicated than that of a non-communist country, which usually consists of a single Ministry of Defence, or ministries for the army, navy and air force, having some dockyards and arsenals of their own (plus nuclear establishments in the case of the four Nuclear Powers), but relying in the main upon contracts with private firms for the manufacture of aricraft, ships and the whole *material* of war. In the Soviet Union the state itself undertakes the production of all arms and equipment, both nuclear and conventional; and there is a duality of the ruling Communist Party and state organisations at every level. Thus the whole of the arms industry, probably the largest in the world, forms an important part of the planned economy. The duality of state and Party functions is most clearly demonstrated in Mr Leonid Brezhnev himself, who is General Secretary of the Communist Party of the Soviet Union, Chairman of its Politburo, which is the policy-making body, and of the Defence Council, President of the Presidium of the Supreme Soviet, Commander-in-Chief of the Armed Forces and a Marshal of the Soviet Union to boot. Stalin himself enjoyed the same concentration of power, but no accusation of personal tyranny is made against Mr Brezhnev who, by all accounts, respects the distinctive functions of his departments and aims at reaching decisions in the Politburo on the basis of general agreement. It seems probable, therefore, that when he retires or goes to his reward, there will be a period of collective leadership without any dramatic alteration in the policies which he has developed.

The real oligarchy of the Soviet Union is about three-hundred in number and of these some forty constitute the military leadership. They are (according to the latest 1979 list) almost all old men by comparison with the service chiefs of other countries. Only nine are under sixty years old. The Minister of Defence, Marshal D.F. Ustinov, promoted by Mr Brezhnev in 1977 to succeed the late Marshal Gretchkho, is seventy-two, so is General V.F. Margelov, Commander of Airborne Forces, while Marshal K.S. Moskalenko, Inspector General, is seventy-seven. Admiral of the Fleet S.G. Gorshkov, who has been Commander-in-Chief of the Navy since 1956 is sixty-eight. The benefit of experience seems largely to outweigh encouragement to promotion.

THE COMMUNIST PARTY AND DEFENCE POLICY

In the field of defence as in internal affairs, the Party is the master. The Ministers of Defence and Foreign Affairs as well as General Yu. V. Andropov, the Chairman of the KGB, are members of the Politburo. There is in addition a Defence Council, also a Party body, which appears to be small in number. This may be, in effect, the defence committee of the Politburo, as it consists of a few leading members of that body and the Party

Secretary responsible for Defence Industry, together with the Chief of the General Staff and other Deputy Defence Ministers, as required. The Politburo itself is the nearest equivalent to our Cabinet — though it is not a state organ. It is supported by the personal staff of the General Secretary of the Party and its Central Committee.

> The Central Committee has three departments which deal with Defence matters. The Main Political Administration (which is also an important branch of the Ministry of Defence) is concerned primarily with the morale and political state of the Armed forces; the Administrative Organs department deals mainly with personnel matters; the Department of Defence Industry has responsibility for military production.[6]

There has been a tendency in recent years to bring into being Institutes of the Academy of Science to fulfil functions not unlike those of the Rand Corporation in the United States or the International Institute of Strategic Studies in London, the Institute of World Economy and International Relations, for instance, and the Institute of the United States and Canada. The Central Committee uses the advice of such bodies as these in preparing the policy decisions of the Politburo. Such in brief outline is the involvement of the higher echelons of the Communist Party in the formulation of Defence Policy.

THE ADMINISTRATIVE MECHANISM OF DEFENCE

The actual machinery of government with its huge cumbersome bureaucracy, complicated by the interaction of All-Union and Republic authorities, and the armed forces themselves have tasks not dissimilar to those of other countries. The Council of Ministers seems, however, to be mainly concerned nowadays with economic and social affairs, leaving other questions of policy to the Foreign and Defence Ministers to cope with in the Politburo, except for two important aspects of defence. The Council is concerned with the Management of military research and development; and one of its Deputy Chairmen, Mr L.V. Smirnov, is head of the Military Industrial Commission which co-ordinates the whole process of weapons procurement under the direction of the Party Secretary for the Defence Industry. Mr David Holloway, who is our best-informed guide on the subject in this country[7] writes:

> Production and R. and D. are carried out chiefly in the research institutes, design bureaux and factories of various production ministries — in particular the nine Ministries in the Defence Industry group (see below). The Defence sector enjoys special priority in the economy and this helps it to perform more effectively than civilian industry. The operation of the defence sector imposes its own pattern of design and development on Soviet weapons policies.

The Defence Ministry itself is an immense apparatus. The High Command consists of the Minister himself, Marshal Ustinov, and three First Deputy Defence Ministers, the Commander-in-Chief of the Warsaw Pact, Marshal V.G. Kulikov, the Chief of the General Staff, General N.V. Ogarkov, and Marshal S.L. Sokolov. Next come ten Deputy Defence Ministers, the Commander-in-Chief Strategic Missile Forces, General V.F. Tolubko; Admiral of the Fleet S.G. Gorshkov, Commander-in-Chief of the Navy and the other Commanders-in-Chief of Ground Forces, the Air-Defence Command and Soviet Air Forces; the Chief Inspector; the Chief of Rear Services; the Chief of Billeting and Construction; the Chief of Civil Defence; the Deputy Minister for Weapons Production, and General A.D. Yepishev, Chief of the Main Political Administration (MPA). In addition to these Ministerial posts, twenty-two full Generals and two Senior Admirals belong to the High Command Group. They include the Chairman of the KGB, the Chief of Staff of the Warsaw Pact, the Naval Chief of Staff, 1st Deputy Commanders, the Heads of Military Academies and the Commanders of some of the more important Military Districts, at present Moscow, Kiev, Trans-Baikal, Central Asia, Baltic, Far Eastern and Carpathian. The expertise of these professional fighting men and their staffs, in the midst of party politicians and bureaucrats, gives them great influence in shaping the general military policy of the Soviet Union as well as the planning and conduct of operations and the whole range of arms procurement.

Plans and orders for the manufacture of weapons and equipment, including those of the strategic nuclear force, prepared by the High Command have, of course, to be cleared with the Defence Council and the Politburo itself and co-ordinated with *Gosplan*, the central planning agency.

The Arms Industry

There are eight Defence Industry Ministries, all under Ministers who are also members of the Central Committee of the Party. They are the Ministries of the Aviation Industry; the Defence Industry; the General Machinery Industry; the Machinery Industry; the Means of Communication Industry; the Medium Machinery Industry; the Radio—Technical Industry and the Shipbuilding Industry. Listed with this group of Ministries is the State Committee for the Peaceful Use of Atomic Energy. There must, of course, be a very large establishment for the development and production of nuclear missiles and bombs. No separate ministry for this task if officially listed; it may be assumed that the Deputy Ministers of Defence responsible for the Strategic Missile Forces and Weapons Production are included. Of the Ministries listed above the functions of the Aviation and Shipbuilding Ministries are clear; the latter, if it includes the Merchant Marine and Fishing Fleets as well as warships, must be an immense undertaking. The Ministry of Radio—Technical Industry, no doubt, directs the production of radio, radar, space satellites and all the requirements of electronic warfare.

How the functions of the three Machinery Ministries and the Ministry of Defence Industry are distinguished from one another is obscure. Which, for instance, is responsible for the mass production of armoured fighting vehicles and which for artillery? There must be a vast quantity of material and equipment needed for the fighting services (e.g. boots, clothing, protection against nuclear radiation and chemical warfare) which do not seem to come within the scope of these Ministries. The search for information on the real costs of armaments and the fighting forces is no more enlightening. Alec Nove in the latest edition of his classical works *The Soviet Economic System* has this to say:

It is interesting to speculate where defence expenditure appears. Pay and subsistence of military personnel is evidently in 'consumption'. But what about weapons and current expenses such as fuel used in vehicles? The latter would be in 'material consumption in institutions serving the population', along with items which fit this sub-head better, such as the feeding of patients in hospitals, the use of school books, etc. Perhaps the weapons (or the increase in weapons) most logically belong under 'increase in inventories and reserves'. There is another table in the statistical annual which separates out defence within the national income total, but on a closer examination the figure is simply the budgetary defence vote which does not help us in the present instance.

We are therefore thrown back upon guesswork, upon which American Intelligence experts have spent a great deal of time, to reach a realistic estimate of the financial cost of the greatest military force in the world. Since the whole financial system of the Communist state, based on Marxist principles which disregard, or absorb in social functions, so many factors of the cost of operations, is completely different from the income and expenditure system of non-Communist states, we are never likely to obtain a comprehensible picture of it. Only where hard currencies are needed to pay for imports do we enter a field in which transactions can be measured in terms of dollars or other exchangeable currencies. Purchases of machines and industrial technology certainly are an important feature of Soviet expenditure, but, though they may be indirectly of military utility, there is no means of computing the part which they play in Defence Expenditure. The CIA reckon the Soviets' defence expenditure, including weapons, at twelve to thirteen per cent of the GNP, which in 1978 was estimated to be equivalent to $617 billion. A better guide to the impact of this great concentration on preparations for war upon the Soviet population is to determine the number of people employed in the armaments industry in addition to the 4 800 000 men under arms. Here again exact figures are not available; but some forty per cent of the whole labour force of the Soviet Union, over thirteen million, that is, is employed in the machine-making and machine-working industries, of which arms production is a major part.

There is a sense, therefore, in which we can describe the Soviet Union as a whole as a war machine. It is not indeed that the Russian people as a whole has any desire for war. It is because all the resources of society — manpower, institutions, industry and the whole apparatus for the formation and manipulation of ideas — are so organised that they could very quickly be mobilised by the all-powerful political oligarchy, if it judged the moment ripe for an onslaught upon the weakening capitalist world.

8 Soviet armaments: present strength

CONVENTIONAL FORCES: LAND AND AIR.

Admiral of the Fleet, Lord Hill-Norton, when he retired from post of Chairman of the Military Committee of NATO at the end of 1977, summarised as follows the actual strength of the Soviets' conventional land and air forces in Europe in his book *No Soft Options*.[1]

They [the Soviets] have failed, and we all share the expectation that they will continue to fail, to win the battle of ideas. Therefore their aim, if it is to be achieved, will only be achieved by naked armed power. And it is here that we so clearly see what is happening — the relentless determination to pile military might on military might until political pressure, threats or blackmail will win their game without recourse to war to all. And this is the threat — or better the challenge — which we must meet or go under. It is unnecessary to quote long lists of figures, but some facts must be quoted to give substance to these assertions. The Warsaw Pact has half a million more men under arms than it had ten years ago, and some thirty more divisions; their total holding of tanks has risen in the same period from 47 000 to 60 000 and their factories are turning out at least 3000 more each year. In Allied Command Europe, in broad terms, their superiority in conventional strength is not far removed from the three to one ratio that has been quoted as the classical requirement for successful offence.

And their gigantic fleet of tank-transporters, their mobile bridging equipment, their heavy self-propelled artillery and their greatly improved machinery for rapid reinforcement all add to their offensive potential in a way it is impossible to ignore.

The Admiral goes on to record the superiority of the Soviet Union in terms of tactical in-place aircraft in the Central Region of Europe and two factors which have significantly increased their air power.

> First, modern technology has given them far greater range and hitting power; they can carry four times the payload ten times as far as in the 1950s. The second factor is their switch from a largely defensive configuration of their combat aircraft to an offensive one, as a result of which the massive re-equipment with multi-role aircraft over the last few years now allows the Soviet commander to use almost all his force in an offensive role.

This immense and continuous increase of conventional armaments and the no-less incessant development of nuclear power so far exceeds any possible defensive needs that we look for any rational explanation of it on the Soviet side. If there were in the Soviet Union any body of opinion comparable to that which exists in non-Communist countries, the fact that some twelve or thirteen per cent of the GNP of a far from affluent society is being spent for military purposes would raise a great deal of criticism. But there is none; and, except for the very limited influence of foreign broadcasts, the Soviet citizen has no information to counteract the official Party doctrine and propaganda about the international situation of the Soviet Union and the purpose of its armed forces.

Two strands are evident in the prevailing propaganda — nationalism and a kind of ideological xenophobia. Ever since Stalin called upon the old love of country in order to rally the Russians to resist the Nazi invader, the 'Great Patriotic War' has been the point of departure of all modern history teaching in the schools and an inspiration for national pride. However cosmopolitan and ideological the formulations of policy by the CPSU we find plenty of references in the speeches and writings of the Soviet leaders about the armed forces to 'our country'. Add to this that it has been a Russian tradition from the time of Peter the Great that national defence requires an army greater than that of any potential enemy, and we have a natural disposition to accept, as a fact of life, the all-round superiority of the Soviet Union's armaments. The second strand, inherent in the Communist doctrine of incessant *struggle* against the capitalists is the notion, sedulously fostered, that foreign countries, surrounding the Socialist fatherland, are intrinsically hostile; this applies particularly to the United States and, in Europe, to the German *revanchists*, as they are called. No doubt the idea of drawing the teeth of the capitalists and advancing the patriotic and socialist cause without war, through *détente* and the policy of Peaceful Coexistence, is appreciated by the more sophisticated; but the plan of frustrating their knavish tricks with the threat of the Soviet Union's own nuclear power is, I should guess, more appealing.

There would seem, therefore, to be no internal forces within the Soviet Union to restrain the determination of the Politburo to use military strength to the maximum to promote its ambitions, unless economic difficulties within the Union itself, and in its relations with satellite states, become much more serious than they are at present.

Let us look now at some of the principal features of the Soviet military array in 1981. There are 1 825 000 men in the army which has 47 tank divisions, 118 motorised rifle divisions and 8 airborne divisions. Of these Category 1 divisions — that is, of three quarters to full strength with complete equipment — 3 are deployed in Eastern Europe outside the Soviet Union itself. The armed forces of those members of the Warsaw Pact, who might be involved in the event of hostilities with NATO, have a total strength of 674 500 and include 13 tank divisions. Of the 60 000 tanks of which Lord Hill Norton writes, 20 500 main battle tanks in operational service are in Northern and Central Europe as against NATO's 7000. Of these the tanks of the Soviet Union's own forces will almost certainly be by 1981 the latest types, the T72s, while their allies may have a number of the earlier models (T62, T59). The T72, the principal conventional offensive weapon which confronts the variety of battle tanks of the Atlantic Alliance weights 40 tons, carries a 125 mm smooth-bore gun, is equipped with a laser range-finder and has a maximum speed of 70 km/h. It has a crew of three.

In Southern Europe the Warsaw Pact has 6700 tanks against 4000 of the Atlantic Allies. The Soviet Union has also an abundance of other armoured fighting vehicles (55 000 according to 1978 figures) including the BMP mechanised infantry combat vehicles which enable the infantry to go into action as fast as the tanks. Their anti-tank guns and guided missiles have their counterpart in the NATO forces but are far more numerous. Of the Soviets' total of 20 000 artillery pieces, 10 800, towed or self-propelled, are classified as anti-tank weapons. They have also 9000 AA guns, six varieties of mobile surface-to-air missile systems and about 1300 launchers of nuclear-capable surface-to-surface missiles (FROG, Scud, Scaleboard). How many of these are on the central and northern Fronts, on the southern, in the Military Districts of the Soviet Union itself, or on the Chinese frontier we are not told, but it is estimated that there is a ratio of three guns and mortars to one between the Warsaw Pact and NATO forces.

Comparisons of combat manpower are particularly difficult owing to the different kinds of military organisations on either side. The representatives of NATO countries involved with those of the Warsaw Pact in the long-drawn discussions at Vienna on Mutual Force Reductions have insisted upon taking the total number of men serving in the armies and air forces of the two sides in the Central European area as the most practical basis of comparison, their object being to arrive by stages at parity between the two. Prolonged objections on the Soviet side to the basis of calculation held up agreement, but according to Western estimates the total of Warsaw Pact forces in that area is 962 000. The ground forces available without mobilisation or reinforcement to the two sides in Europe, reckoned in 'divisional equivalents'[2] by the International Institute for Strategic Studies, are in Central and Northern Europe twenty-seven available to NATO — or thirty including the French divisions deployed in Germany — and forty-seven to the Warsaw Pact, and in Southern Europe thirty-seven to NATO (including the separate Italian, Greek and Turkish armies) and twenty-one to the Warsaw Pact. The vital difference, in comparing combat manpower on the outbreak of hostilities, depends upon the speed and volume of reinforcement. Here the Soviet Union and its allies, operating on interior lines and having large standing conscript forces in close proximity to the probable battle area, have an immense advantage. The reinforcing formations available to the Warsaw Pact are reckoned at one hundred and fifteen and a half 'div. equivalents', those available to the Atlantic Alliance, including France, at fifty-two and a half.

Such in broad outline is the position regarding the rival land forces in Europe, the salient features of which are the numerical superiority of the Soviet bloc in armour and gunnery and its ability to expand its forces by swift reinforcement. The imponderables are the quality of weapons and of leadership. What of the air? The number of tactical aircraft of the Warsaw Pact has increased by about 1300 since 1972. They had (in mid-1979) 4200 central and northern Europe compared with NATO's 2350 and 1595 in southern Europe compared with 940 of NATO. The co-operation of French squadrons in the event of war would add 400–500 good fighters to the strength of the Atlantic Alliance.

On the side of the Warsaw Pact it is believed that the growing number of new multi-role fighter-bombers designed for deep strike and interdiction, including the MiG-27 Flogger, the Su 17/20 Fitter, and the Su-19 Fencer, are reserved for the Soviet Union's Air Force itself, while the older machines designed for a defensive rôle are supplied to the satellite air forces. Here, while there is disparity in numbers, there is none in quality. The United States F-15, A-10 and F-111 and the British Tornado, for instance, have, like their Soviet rivals, the latest laser-guided missiles and other precision-guided weapons and all the gadgetry of electronic warfare. The Soviet Air Force has 3400 helicopters; they are greatly outnumbered by those of the US Air Force, though how many of each are normally deployed in the European theatre is not clear. Just as the capacity to reinforce land forces in large numbers from interior lines gives the Soviets the edge over an alliance of separate countries with different systems of military service and with its main source of additional manpower and material 3000 miles away across the Atlantic, so an air force having — as has the Soviets — a great depth of territory in the rear in which to locate its airfields, operational, repair and refuelling bases, has the advantage over air forces cramped for space in the narrow and overcrowded zone of western Europe. The English airfields are the only staging bases for trans-Atlantic reinforcement. The withdrawal of France from NATO (but not the Alliance) has deprived the NATO powers of the automatic right to use French airfields. Permission to do so would have to be granted specifically in times of war.

THE EXPANDING NAVY

The Soviet Navy, consisting almost entirely of very modern ships, is now the second largest in the world and has far more submarines than any other navy. Why? While building it the Soviet Union had no overseas territorial responsibilities, no foreign sources of energy and raw materials or commercial interests of sufficient importance to justify such vast expenditure. Admiral of the Fleet Sergei Gorshkov, himself the architect of this tremendous achievement, gives the answer in his book *The Sea Power of the State*.[3] 'Soviet sea power, merely a minor defensive arm in 1953, has become the optimum means to defeat the imperialist enemy and the most important element in the Soviet arsenal to prepare the way for a Communised world.'

He is a great believer in Engels' description of the navy as 'the political force at sea' and, in an article in *Morskoi Sbornik* wrote: 'The flag of the Soviet Navy now flies over the oceans of the world. Sooner or later the West will have to understand that it is no longer master of the seas.'

To achieve this global purpose the Soviet Navy needs bases further afield than the traditional home ports of its four fleets, Murmansk, Leningrad, Odessa and Vladivostok, and it is mostly by filling the vacuum created by the liquidation of the French, British and Portuguese Empires that it has found what it needs.

In the Atlantic it had for some years had a naval and air reconaissance base at Conakry, the use of which was reported to be suspended in 1980 by the Government of Guinea. But since the Portuguese revolution, it has strengthened its position in that area through the use of the Cape Verde archipelago and some useful docks at Bissau. On the opposite Western side of the Atlantic Ocean, Cuba, now a member of Comecon, and a main source of military manpower for the new revolutionary imperialism, provides every facility and is the basis for any operations to be undertaken in the Caribbean. Further South on the African side, Luanda and Lobito are good harbours now in Communist hands. In the Indian Ocean Mabuto, Beira and Nacala are of similar utility and, at the mouth of the Red Sea, Aden, now in the People's Republic of Yemen, has already been converted into a well-equipped submarine base. The Indian Ocean islands, notably Madagascar, Mauritius and the Seychelles, now in Left-wing hands, provide docking and refuelling facilities for the auxiliary fishing fleet. In the Pacific the disused bases of the US Navy in Vietnam will be available as required. There are on average forty Soviet naval ships at any one time in the Mediterranean.

The total tonnage of the navies of the Atlantic Alliance, with 434 major surface combat ship,[4] is much greater than that of the Soviets with 275 such vessels, but most of the European Allies' fleets are necessarily committed to defence in their own home waters. In ocean-wide operations, for which the quickly growing Soviet Navy is mainly designed, it is really only the United States Navy and the Royal Navy that can be regarded as its strategic rivals.

The powerful French Navy shares with the Italian and the American 6th Fleet the burden of Mediterranean defence. The surface strength of the Soviet Navy consists of two Kiev class aircraft carriers, equipped with vertical or short-take-off-and-landing aircraft, large anti-submarine helicopters and short and long-range guided missiles, a battle-cruiser and two Moskva helicopter cruisers, 16 missile-armed anti-submarine cruisers, 11 conventional cruisers, 80 destroyers, 97 ocean escorts, 150 supply and repair ships and over 1000 smaller warships. The shorebased naval air force consists of 870 combat aircraft, of which the supersonic *Backfire* bombers, equipped for either conventional or nuclear missions, are the most formidable.

The United States Navy alone, with its thirteen huge aircraft carriers, a surface fleet which includes twenty-nine guided weapon cruisers, thirty-five ASW cruisers, thirty-five destroyers and sixty-five frigates and a large naval airforce, is more than a match for the Soviet surface fleet. But it is the Soviets' nuclear submarine force which gives it a marked superiority over all its potential opponents, and constitutes the main danger to the maritime lines of communication of the Atlantic Allies. The Soviet Union at present has 1028 submarine-launched ballistic missiles in ninety nuclear-powered submarines — and there are more building; in addition there are eighty-four nuclear-powered boats, half of which are equipped with tactical nuclear weapons. Apart from this large contribution to the Soviets' nuclear armoury which we have next to consider, they have some other 150 diesel-propelled submarines.

The comparable NATO figures of SLBMs are, United States six hundred and fifty-six in forty-one submarines; United Kingdom sixty-four in four submarines; France sixty-four in four, with two more boats to carry sixteen SBLM's each now building. These three powers have in addition eighty-two attack submarines. Anti-submarine warfare has the highest priority on both sides.

SOVIET NUCLEAR ARMS

It is with the balance of strategic nuclear strength between the two super-powers that American expert commentators, whose name is legion and particularly the 'arms-control community' are almost exclusively concerned. But I have put first the great build-up of conventional forces by the Warsaw Pact not only because it has been historically the task of NATO to organise a sufficient defence against them; but also because I believe that even now the Soviets might consider a massive offensive without their taking the initiative of using nuclear weapons preferable to inviting the inevitable American riposte to the use of them. For there can be no telling how the Soviet people would react, however efficient the measures of civil defence, to the massive destruction caused by even a few ballistic missiles which is quite a different matter to the patriotic defence of the national territory against an invader. On one point at least of the famous Policy of Peaceful Coexistence we must all agree. 'The main thing is to ward off a thermo-nuclear war; to prevent it breaking out.' The notion that the initial use of tactical nuclear weapons by the Warsaw Pact, to which NATO would certainly retort in kind, could lead to a duel restricted to that level is theoretically conceivable; it is more probable that it would quickly escalate to an exchange of medium and inter-mediate range missiles, which already means the destruction of centres of population far greater than that of Hiroshima and Nagasaki. It is, perhaps, slightly more probable that, the nuclear devastation of Western Europe and western cities of the Soviet Union having reached that stage, the ultimate escalation to the exchange of strategic ballistic missiles between the Soviet Union and the United States might be forsworn. But the escalation doctrine written into NATO's pattern of 'flexible response' has, as we have seen in an earlier chapter, no counterpart in the Soviets' empirical military planning.

It is only the intercontinental missiles of the two super-powers which were limited in number by the SALT I Treaty and are intended to be fixed at levels of equivalence by SALT II, if it is ever ratified. At present the Soviet Union has 2507 delivery venicles, ICBMs, SLBMs and strategic bombers — as against the United States 2097, but the Americans have a much larger number of independent warheads on their missiles, 7274, to the Soviets' 2970. The intention of the SALT II Treaty was to level off the total of delivery vehicles retained by both signatories at 2250 of which 1320 would be MIRV missiles or aircraft with cruise missiles (CMs). A protocol intended to last till 1980, but now probably defunct, would ban the deployment of mobile ICBM launchers and sea or land-launched CMs of a range over 600 km. The throw-weight, however, of the Soviets' ICBM monsters was not to be limited by the Treaty, which is one of the reasons why the Armed Forces Committee of the US Senate so strongly criticised it.

Evidence that the Soviet High Command takes the prospect of nuclear attack seriously is given in the *Military Balance 1979—80* of the IISS.

Strategic defence is provided by extensive air-defence radars, SAM interceptors and the Moscow ABM complex of 64 launchers. Considerable effort is being devoted to defence against the American air-launched cruise missile threat which will develop in the 1980s. It is believed that research is continuing on anti-satellite and exotic technologies which may have application for ballistic missile defence.

In estimating the nuclear systems capable of operation in the European theatre the IISS includes, as well as the land-based intermediate, medium and short-range ballistic missiles and land-based aircraft of the Warsaw Pact, submarine-launched missiles assumed to be deployed in the Baltic; and on the side of the Atlantic Alliance the French and British SLBMs, the French land-based IRBM and carrier-based aircraft in range, as well as land-based nuclear-capable aircraft. To the latter United States Poseidon missiles allocated to SACEUR are added. This adds up to a total inventory of 5364 on the Warsaw Pact side and 2045 on the side of the Atlantic Allies. In addition to the Soviets' mobile SS20, they have eight other types of land-based missiles deployed with 2244 warheads assumed available, whereas NATO has as yet only the Pershing 1, the range of which is too short to reach the Soviet Union. Its total available warheads come to 1811.

President Carter's decision, endorsed by the North Atlantic Council, to meet this threat by stationing a force of long-range Pershing 2s in Germany and 500 cruise missiles in England and Italy will go far to redress the balance. It will provide NATO Europe with an American nuclear umbrella which is rather more credible than the strategic inter-continental umbrella. But it would be three or four years before the promised Pershings and cruise missiles can be in position, while the mass of Soviet launching systems, which I have listed above, deployed in Western Russia and beyond the Urals, have their missiles trained on Western Europe — Britain included. That is the measure of our immediate danger.

SATELLITES AND ELECTRONIC WARFARE

A many-sided space programme has been developed in the Soviet Union during the last two decades and nothing fires popular interest and national pride more than the achievements of manned space-ships. Though exact figures are not published, it is certain that satellites play an important part in Soviet military planning for photographic reconnaissance, eaves-dropping on conversations and orders, often in co-operation with ships and aircraft specially equipped for spying (e.g. off the Atlantic Coast of America), and for electronic warfare. They would un-doubtedly be used, in war, to intercept and destroy opponents' satellites. The large Soviet satellite *Kosmos 954* which crashed and disintegrated in the North of Canada in January 1978 made it possible to judge the extent of Soviet expertise in this field. Of this, Colonel E. Asa Bates Jr., US Air Force writes in the *RUSI Journal*:[5]

> Kosmos 954 was a three-sectional, 45 ft. long reconnaissance satellite of a type that the Soveit Union had been launching for a decade to track American naval vessels. The 1,000 lb. nuclear reactor aboard the 6,000 lb. satellite was used to generate electricity that powered an ocean-scanning radar, which tracked surface ships and radios, and which beamed data back to Soviet ground stations about the number and position of the vessels.

The same writer quotes a 1976 report on Soviet space recon-naissance projects that

> spy satellites are the largest single element in a space-launching programme that is many times as active as the American one.

The latest estimate reveals that over the past five years the Soviet Union has launched 325 satellites, presumed for military purposes. The American total during that period has been reported as 48.

The Americans in fact rely on large multi-purpose satellites of the *Big Bird* variety which remain in orbit longer than most of the Soviets'. It is not certain which of the many Soviet satellites in the Cosmos series are used for gathering electronic intelligence data.

In the *Table of Earth*, published by the Royal Air Force Establishment, a large number of Soviet satellites, ellipsoidal in shape and weighing about 400 kg. are listed; and it is estimated that of these, those from Plesetsk (the Russian equivalent of Cape Canavaral) are possibly electronic reconnaissance satellites.[6]

Most of their naval vessels and many of their aircraft are also equipped with electronic warfare devices to detect and confuse enemy radar and cope with electronic countermeasures. In this field, as in the use of computers, there is reason to believe that the Atlantic Allies, including the British, have a measure of technical superiority.

9 Prospects of the projection of Soviet power

What are likely to be the uses to which the great military potential of the Soviet Union is put in the next decade? This is a matter of pure speculation. All that can reasonably be attempted is to define, as expert students of Soviet policy and military doctrine have done, the ideological and strategic principles and the Russian legacy which can be assumed to determine the actions of the CPSU, and so to judge what is improbable or probable.[1]

We must start with the premise that the governing principle of the Soviet Union, which distinguishes it from almost all other countries outside its orbit, is not static, but dynamic; its *raison d'être*, as sufficiently illustrated already in these pages, is to promote the world revolution, of which it is itself the core. Of one thing, therefore, we can be sure; that the Soviet Union and its military authorities will not contemplate with satisfaction the maintenance of the *status quo* for a decade or more. Having so secure a base and military superiority in Europe, it is logical to suppose that they will look for opportunities to project their power in other continents.

If progress towards Communism can be made in any country by internal means without any military intervention, so much the better. It is indeed the purpose of the 'Policy of Peaceful Coexistence' to favour this process, represented, whether or not it involves violent disturbance, as a phase of the class war against the capitalists. There is no state which is immune from this sapping and undermining. The Portuguese 'Revolution' of 1974 is a classical example of it — and a striking example, also, of how such an attempt to seize power can be thwarted when a majority of the people is able to assert its will. To this same process belong the many *coups* which have been attempted periodically in various unstable states of Latin America; the persistence of Communist militants in starting and prolonging the strikes which paralyse the industries of the Western democracies; assistance to political terrorists; the orchestration of anti-nuclear protests and demonstrations hostile to the Atlantic Alliance etc. All this involves the attention of the Agitation and Propaganda mechanism of the CPSU in co-operation with indigenous Communist parties and fellow-travellers. It does not concern the Armed Forces of the Soviet Union, except in the sense of a common ideological purpose.

The possible operations of those forces outside the frontiers of the Soviet Union and the Warsaw Pact fall into two categories: (1) major wars, which could only be against NATO or China (or conceivably, both); (2) minor wars designed to bring lesser states into the Socialist network, preferably by assistance to local revolutions.

It is the former which almost monopolises attention in the Western countries, since it concerns their immediate security and accounts, most obviously, for the vast accumulation of conventional armaments and nuclear weapons by the Russians. War between the Soviet Union and China is always a possibility also, though it would not be to the manifest advantage of either of the two great Communist rivals. Whatever its issue, it would be bound to have a weakening effect on the Russians, which could only benefit the Western Alliance, as does the present necessity of keeping forty-six Soviet Divisions on the Eastern frontier. This itself is not without importance as a deterrent to the risk of starting a major offensive against the West.

No-one can say that the Third World War, which is so widely feared and so knowingly forecast, will not occur. But it is at least arguable that in the present circumstances it is less likely than a series of ventures to extend the Socialist domain, with military assistance, in what is called the third world. Here also the projection of the rapidly expanding Soviet maritime power will depend upon whether or not it is liable, in one sea-area or another, to provoke active opposition from the United States and its allies. I say less likely; for, if a general war broke out between the Soviet Union and NATO, it could be no other than the great (and presumably final) 'showdown' with the Capitalists. I should doubt, if I were a revolutionary convinced of the eventual triumph of Communism, whether the time for the ultimate duel had yet arrived, for military and political victory appears too uncertain.

What would happen after the Deluge also does not seem to be

clear to the Soviet seer. The official argument that the Soviet Union could win and outlive a nuclear war — and its military manuals have definite plans for the control of the enemy's surviving population — is all very well; but how much of the industrial world would there be left to socialize? We have, too, Marshal Sokolowsky's conclusion (see p. 49) that, if things go well enough with the 'world socialist camp', war will not be inevitable. Without therefore arguing for any relaxation in the efforts of the West to prepare for a major offensive by the Warsaw Pact in Europe, I suggest that more attention be given to the prospect during the next few years of operations designed to extend the area of Soviet power in other parts of the world, as has already been done with considerable success during the 1970s in South East Asia, Africa and Southern Arabia.

So far as the projection of Russian military force as an instrument of expansion is concerned, geography establishes a basic distinction between the practical possibilities of action against or within countries contiguous to the territory of the Soviet Union or its satellites and the rest. Peter Vigor neatly sums up the situation:

> with the exception of Finland, Austria, Yugoslavia, Iran, Afghanistan, India and Pakistan, Third World countries are not directly accessible to the USSR. In other words, if she wants to wage a war against any one of them, . . . she has got to cross the seas or indulge in airlifts in order to be able to do it.[2]

If we begin by considering the countries accessible by land, invasion of Finland or Austria is improbable, the former, already bound to the Soviet Union by a defence agreement, because outright annexation would almost inevitably involve war with Sweden; the latter because the neutrality of Austria suits the Soviet purpose as a model for German neutralisation. More serious are the opportunities for expansion in the area of the Persian Gulf. Since the above words were published in 1979, Afghanistan has already been occupied by Soviet troops and the Western Alliance, despite its protestations and the United Nations' condemnation of the invasion of an independent unaligned country, has been unable to do anything about it. Intervention in Iran, beginning with economic and technical aid at the invitation of the government, to replace the losses caused by the sanctions imposed by the United States and its allies and developing into military assistance to the Tudeh Party to seize power, would seem to be a possible move. One of the worst consequences of the humiliating failure of the United States to rescue the American hostages from the Iranians, and of the vey understandable refusal of their allies, despite their moral support, to consider any military means to achieve that end, is the effect upon the Yugoslav situation of this reluctance of the West to take risks. For it has generally been held that, while the Russians, now that Tito has died, would undoubtedly wish, for ideological and strategic reasons to reunite Yugoslavia with the Soviet bloc of Communist states in Europe, the Atlantic Alliance would be ready to fight to protect its independence. The strengthening of Yugoslavia's links with the European Economic Community implied a similar desire of the Western Europeans to reinforce its freedom. It is indeed vital to the defence of NATO in the whole Mediterrean area that Yugoslavia should not fall into Soviet hands.

OVERSEAS EXPEDITIONS

So much for the danger of the military and political expansion of Soviet power into neighbouring neutral or unaligned countries in Europe and Western Asia. The process of projecting armed forces across the sea is a very different matter. Unlike all the other Empires which have come and gone — Spanish, Portuguese, British, French, Dutch, American — and, for a short period, Belgian, German and Italian — Russia had never extended its possessions by planting colonies or annexing land overseas. Its imperial expansion had always been on land with the solitary exception of the extension of discoveries in the Far East of Asia into Alaska. Consequently there is no tradition of colonial service in the Russian army and navy as there is in the regiments and naval establishments of the other ex-imperialists of Europe. It is only as a peripheral adjunct to a major campaign that the transporting of a special military force by ship, or, since the Second World War, by air, finds its place in Soviet military manuals. But it is an important place. The operation is known as a *desant* and its traditional aim is to get one's troops into the enemy's flank or rear. There were many examples of this in the Second World War

— Arnhem being one that was not very successful — the seizure of Oslo by the Germans in 1940 another. The Russians mounted many of them, both seaborne and airborne, in 1945 against the Japanese, mainly to help capture South Sakhalin and the Kurile Islands. Vigor writes:

> Soviet thinking classifies airborne *desant* into two categories: (i) the tactical: (ii) the operational and strategic. Tactical airborne *desants*, according to Soviet sources, are usually carried out by ordinary motor-rifle units or sub-units. . . . The means of transport for these *desants* is the helicopter. The troops employed are to be landed in the enemy's rear in order to co-operate with their own advancing ground forces; or to destroy the enemy's tactical nuclear weapons and also his command posts and communication centres; or to seize bridges, etc.
>
> On the other hand, airborne *desants* at the operational or strategic level are carried out by the airborne forces proper . . .[3]

Soviet military manuals go into considerable detail about the use of *desants* in different kinds of war, nuclear, conventional or conventional with the limited use of tactical nuclear weapons. Seaborne or airborne *desants* could obviously be employed in a major war against the Atlantic Alliance (e.g. to take Narvik or airfields in Northern Norway); and the vulnerability of the Chinese coasts to this mode of attack accounts for the kind of navy which the Chinese People's Republic has built.

What concerns our study of strategic probabilities in the near future, however, is the use which the Soviet General Staff have made and may be expected to make again of this mode of operation in transporting not Soviet troops, but troops of satellites, with supplies of arms and equipment, to scenes of military intervention outside the Atlantic Treaty Area.

The striking success of two operations of this kind in the 1970s — the Angolan and Ethiopian expeditions — has established the value of the method. In both cases propaganda emphasised that the Soviet Union was helping a 'war of national liberation', though in fact Portugal had given up its sovereignty over Angola, and the Emperor of Ethiopia had been dethroned a good time before these events. The political atmosphere thus created helped to deter the United States or its allies from attempting to arrest the military intervention — as witness the refusal of Congress to sanction Kissinger's effort to support Savimbi's anti-Communist nationalist forces in Angola. There had for many years been small numbers of Cuban soldiers sent to fight with the anti-Portuguese guerrillas, particularly in Guinea, and Castro was very ready to cut a figure in Africa as a leader of the World Revolution. It soon proved therefore that the Soviets could get away with moving an expeditionary force of Cuban troops by sea to Conakry, then Pointe Noire, then Luanda itself so soon as their clients, the MPLA had seized control of it, without the American Navy daring to stop them.

It was for the Russians a welcome contrast to the United States naval blockade of Cuba which followed the missile crisis in 1962. There had been a supply of Soviet arms by air on a small scale to several of the guerrilla forces in Africa before the Portuguese collapse. It was not difficult to expand this process on a large scale and to send transport planes, loaded with tanks, troop carriers, guns, mortars, SAMs, land mines and small arms in profusion, to land at the airfields of Luanda and Henrique de Carvalho. It must be remembered that leaders of the MPLA, like other insurgent leaders in Guinea and Mozambique (Neto, Amilcar Cabral, Dos Santos) had been members of the Portuguese Communist Party for the last twenty years at least, and were familiar, therefore, with the whole scheme of Cunhal and the Russians for precipitating revolution through the Armed Forces Movement and the consequent design for communist control of the Overseas Provinces. In short, it is a mistake to assume that the Soviet-aided Communist take-over was something that just happened out of the blue. What was novel about it was: (1) the lifting of military support for a supposedly native liberation war across the seas, in contrast to the Red Army's intervention on such a pretext in lands adjoining Soviet territory, as in Georgia in 1921 or Eastern Europe in the 1940s, or Afghanistan in 1979; and (2) the use of non-Russian troops for the purpose.

Once the MPLA had got itself into a position where it could proclaim itself to be the government, the question of how many Angolans actually wanted that government could be conveniently ignored, and the Cubans could be brought in to prevent the numerous opponents of that government from giving effective expression to their views by staging a successful counter-coup. Communist media proclaimed that the MPLA represented the 'will of the Angolan People'; and that the Cuban troops were there to ensure that the people's 'will' was respected.

The second basic proposition underlying the Soviet Union's willingness to use force in this particular fashion is that, if the enterprise in question is not certain to be successful, but that if the advantages inherent in it are perceived to be such . . . as to justify the taking of an amount of risk that the Soviet leaders would normally not permit themselves, then *Soviet* troops must not be sent, but those of one of the 'satellites'. This is because the defeat of the latter . . . brings none of the loss of 'face' and collapse of prestige that would be seen to follow the rout of a Soviet battalion.[4]

We have noted on other pages the important strategic gains — naval, economic and political — which the domination of Angola brought to the Soviet Union, with which a treaty of close alliance was very quickly signed.

The success of this original application of the *desant* technique to the seizure of Angola led to the more ambitious operation of the same nature three years later which resulted in the acquisition for the Soviet bloc of the ancient Empire of Ethiopia. Here there was none of the long history of Communist party intrigue which culminated in the takeover of Angola, but rather the rapid exploitation of the ambition of a ruthless military leader, Colonel Megistu Haile-Mariam and his posse of Marxist officers and the establishment of a Communist state as the price of rescuing them from the twin dangers of Somali attacks in the Ogaden and of the Eritrean liberation movements. Compelled by the hostility of the Somalis to abandon their half-built naval and air base at Berbera, the Soviets decided that there was more to gain by backing their Ethiopian opponents. For the choice of this or that national liberation or revolutionary clique (decorated *ad hoc* with the insignia of 'the working class') is, for the CPSU, purely a matter of expediency. This was a much more extensive *desant* than that of Angola. It involved establishing an air-bridge, disregarding the air-space of several intervening states, from the Soviet Union and Bulgaria to Aden as a staging post for the further transport of heavy armaments, vehicles, equipment and troops by air and sea to Ethiopian airfields and ports. Again no Soviet military units as such were involved but a somewhat higher proportion of Soviet officers than Peter Vigor's comment on the Angolan *desant* suggests; the bulk of the combat troops were Cubans, brought by sea and air from other parts of Africa and Cuba itself.

It is not unreasonable to conclude that the success of these two *desants* points the way to the probable projection of Soviet power — the new revolutionary imperialism — in other parts of the world. What parts? There are, of course, always possibilities of intervention in the internal political feuds of this or that African country but, with the addition of Zimbabwe, thanks ironically to British parliamentary procedure, to the long list of Marxist African governments, the strident African liberation campaign of the last twenty years has about reached its term. There remains only the South African citadel of white capitalism, a very hard nut to crack. The economic strength of the South African Republic is such that all the neighbouring African states, Zambia, Malawi, Zimbabwe, Botswana and Mozambique, despite the political postures which their governments assume, are at present quite unable to do without it. Indeed it is difficult to see how the network of railways, port facilities, electric power, food production, mineral exploitation, industrial employment and trade in that area of the continent, which dates from the great era of British development and Portuguese co-operation, can physically be replaced. It is inconceivable that the Soviet rulers have not some definite ideas of how eventually to reduce this stronghold of the capitalists and secure for the 'socialist camp' its mineral wealth and its unique strategic position. They have had great success so far in inhibiting the United States, Britain and Western Europe, from co-operation with South Africa in their own strategic interests by the emotional propaganda of the 'liberation' and 'racist' campaigns, a success to which the obstinate and illiberal policy of *apartheid* has made its contribution.

I doubt whether we shall see any major liberation guerrilla campaigns against the South African Republic mounted from Mozambique, Zimbabwe or Namibia, because of the powerful economic nexus to which I have referred and the efficiency of the South African armed forces; but we can be sure to see increasing

Black demonstrations against government within the country and hostile propaganda from without. This all serves the Soviet purpose; but it seems unlikely that there will be an opportunity for the projection of Soviet military power, vicarious or otherwise, by sea or air in the immediate future.

OPPORTUNITIES IN THE INDIAN OCEAN AND ARABIA

The Organization of African Unity, thanks to the active Marxist elements within it, has been indirectly a useful ally of the Soviet cause in bringing to power governments helpful to the Soviet fleet and its auxiliary trawlers and intelligence vessels in a number of strategically important islands of the Indian Ocean. This is the case of the great island of Madagascar with the former French naval base of Diego Suarez, all the Comoro Islands except Motte, whose link with France still holds, and Mauritius. Thanks to Mr Nyerere and a company of his Tanzanian troops, a Left-wing regime has been installed in the Seychelles. The chief strategic value of these facilities is to provide a background of naval support for a Soviet attempt to control Southern Arabia. It is here that the most promising opportunity for an actual projection of Soviet power exists through the arming and instigation of re-volutionary movements — some already at work — against the con-servative Muslim kingdoms and Sheikdoms of the Arabian peninsula — Saudi Arabia, Oman, Kuwait, Bahrein and the United Emirates of the Gulf. North Yemen and Kuwait are already reported to have turned to the Soviet Union — instead of America — for a supply of arms. For this oil-rich area, the People's Republic of Yemen — with its naval, air, radar and trooping facilities at Aden, is the obvious base of operations. And here the build-up of Cuban reinforcements is already in progress. The Soviet freighter *Leonid Subirov* (21 370 tons), to give an example, sailed from Havana for Aden in February 1980 with 1500 Cuban troops. Where will they go into action? Oman, with the aid of some British officers and airmen, has in recent years successfully fought and defeated a South Yemeni Communist offensive using the Dhofar insurgents. Maybe there will be a second round, for to neutralise Oman would greatly weaken American and British ability to defend their interests in the Gulf.

THE CARIBBEAN FRONT

The other part of the world in which there are great opportunities for Communist expansion is the Caribbean area. Cuba, of course, is the centre of political activity. Cuba is costing the Soviet Union a great deal of money and its economy is in a deplorable state, as the exodus of refugees shows, but Moscow continues to find Castro a worthwhile ally, more useful at the moment for extending its influence than its other close ally, Vietnam, which is at present confined to consolidating its power in Indo-China. Apart from supplying cannon-fodder for Soviet adventures in Africa and the Middle East, Cubans trained by the KGB are now used as conspirators and agitators in most of the Central American States; there are many situations in which the violence of the Right and the contrasts between the wealth of the few and the poverty of the majority play into their hands. The Marxist victory in Nicaragua was the most recent Communist success. Sandenista guerrillas of the National Liberation Front in that country, armed with Soviet weapons by the Cubans, have been captured in El Salvador and they are already active also in Guatemala. The Cuban Communists are having more success in the Central American Republics than their guerrillas had in the Andean Republics since the death of Ché Guevara, and their most striking progress in the last four years has been in the former British West Indies, Guyana, Granada, St Lucia and Domincia. Soviet naval vessels are much in evidence in the Caribbean, especially in Cuban waters, including submarines visiting Cienfuegos, which could quickly be turned into an operational base. Soviet reconnaissance planes with radar, having Cuba as their Southern base, keep shipping off the east coast of the United States under constant surveillance; and, for air and naval control and interception in time of war, Cuba's facilities in the Western Atlantic correspond with those of the Cape Verde Islands, also in Communist hands, in the East.

The real strategic importance to the United States of the Caribbean area — and therefore to the Soviet Union of endangering it — is that it is the receiving basin for the greater part of the Americans' oil from overseas; in fact, seventy-five per cent of the oil imported into the United States passes through the Caribbean.

Much of the crude is refined in the forty-two refineries of the region. The super-tankers do not dock at the US mainland ports, but transfer their cargoes at Trinidad, Curacao or the Virgin Islands into standard-size tankers, which then sail to the eastern or Gulf of Mexico ports of the United States or to the refineries. The oil from Alaska and Ecuador also comes to the Gulf ports through the Pacific—Atlantic pipeline, which runs through the Republic of Panama, or by tanker through the Canal. And, of course, the large output of Venezuelan oil is shipped northward across the Caribbean. This gives some idea of the temptation to the Soviet Union to go as far as possible to transform the Caribbean from the 'American lake' which it has hitherto seemed to be, into a Socialist lake.

10 Propaganda as an instrument of policy

Propaganda — or psychological warfare as the British called it — has become in the mass-media age a common feature of national foreign policy in time of war. But, since the eclipse of Nazi Germany and Fascist Italy, there is no great power of which propaganda is such an ingredient, day in and day out, as it is of the Soviet Union. For, though the Chinese People's Republic is wholly addicted to the Marxist — Leninist dogma, and the rigid conformity of thought which it imposes, it is not so organically committed, as the Russians are, to its world-wide propagation as a weapon of power politics.

Why, one may ask, is it considered necessary by the Communist Party of the Soviet Union to pump the doctrines of materialism, atheism, economic determinism, the class war and the inevitable victory of socialism into every boy and girl, almost from infancy, to indoctrinate continuously every one in school and university, every soldier, sailor and airman, every worker in field or factory, and to stifle any sign of intellectual and scientific independence? There is only one reason; it is because the dogma is fundamentally *unnatural*. It is obliged to fight continuously against the laws and instincts of human nature, moral, social and personal and, in particular, against the bent for freedom which is inherent in the human spirit.

It is only the omnipresent power of the totalitarian state that gives apparent success to the artificial world of Communist dogma. There is no knowing how far the silent majority of Russians has any feeling for it beyond the tacit acceptance of the Establishment. When natural reaction to it is sustained by national and religious tradition, as in Poland or Yugoslavia, most of the generation which has endured thirty years of enforced indoctrination of this kind seems able to shake it off, like water off a duck's back. A compelling objective of the whole, cumbersome

101

machinery of agitation and propaganda in the Soviet Union itself — whether or not the members of the ruling oligarchy really believe in the Marxist — Leninist creed, which is doubtful — is to ensure the unquestioning obedience of the masses in pursuit of the revolutionary imperialism to which that oligarchy is committed.

Communist propaganda is of two sorts; one theoretic, the other practical. In the early days of the Russian Revolution, little distinction was made between the enunciation of the new social gospel, which was expected to carry all before it, and the art of adapting it to specific political and military ends.

'The Third International already has, as its foundation stones, three Soviet Republics, those in Russia, Hungary and Bavaria', Zinovieff wrote in the first number of the review *Kommunisticheski International* which appeared on 1 May 1919.

> But no one will be surprised if, at the moment when these lines appear in print, we have not three but six or more Soviet Republics. Old Europe is dashing at mad speed towards the proletarian revolution. . . . In a year the whole of Europe, will be Communist; and the struggle for Communism will be transferred to America, perhaps to Asia and to other parts of the world.

There was a mood of retreat and disillusionment when it was found that revolution was not just round the corner and that, as Trotsky said, 'History has granted the bourgeoisie a fairly long breathing space.' It was then that Bukharin, editing *Pravda* in Moscow, started on the serious organisation of propaganda through the Comintern. But it is to the period (1924–8) when Stalin decided to concentrate on 'building Socialism in a single country', namely Russia, and its defence against the outer world, that we can trace the origin of the use of Communist propaganda as an organ of national policy. The process went through many phases until it developed, after victory in the Second World War enabled the Soviet Union to break out of its diplomatic and geographical confines, into a powerful weapon of psychological warfare.

As a theoretical system or philosophy, Communism purports to explain, according to laws discovered by Karl Marx and Friederick Engels, the economic history and inevitable development of human society. As such it is advocated, discussed and contested everywhere but particularly in the academic life of the non-Communist world. Here it enjoys freedom of debate, like all political theories; and many are accustomed to think that, wherever Communists have been able by 'constitutional means', as in Italy or France or Greece or Zimbabwe, to win a good many seats in Parliament or to secure a majority of votes in a trade-union election, they are there simply by force of argument. But even in debate, as one knows from experience, what is distinctive about Communists is that they never accept the objective criterion of right or wrong, true or false, just or unjust, by appeal to which members of other political groups endeavour to make their case. Right, to the Communist is simply what advances the revolutionary cause; wrong, what obstructs it; true is what is said by spokesmen of a favoured (say, 'liberation') group anywhere in the world; false what is said by his opponents; just is the demand of 'the workers'; unjust the claim of the 'capitalist'. Nor is there the slightest compunction about lying if it will serve the cause. Theoretic Marxism will always appeal to academics who have no other roots. It has no popular appeal.

Practical Communist propaganda as a deliberate instrument of policy of the Soviet state is another matter and is nowadays of great importance in international politics. We have seen something in earlier chapters of the internal mechanism for ensuring that the various sections of the population are steeped in Communist doctrine; and this remains one of the principal pre-occupations of the Central Committee of the Party.

The only history books available in the schools — and they all base modern history upon the 'Great Patriotic War' — have been rewritten to conform to the Party line. The Komsomol, in which promising boys are enrolled, builds up a core of elite leadership in the Party. The Main Political Administration, as we have seen, ensures indoctrination in every unit of the forces. Neither here nor in any field of Party activity is the requirement of active propaganda neglected, and in every local Party in factory, collective farm, office or institution, there is a member charged with *agit-prop*. *Pravda* is the regular organ of the Party and *Tass* its news agency; these carry the only approved presentation and selection of news about the outer world, and all local newspapers, all magazines and specialised publications, including the military, are also Government-owned and conform to the policies which *Pravda* expresses. *Isvestia* is the official Government paper. In short every kind of education and information is steeped in Communist propaganda and is presented in such a way as to identify the doctrinal slant with national pride and patriotism. The clandestine *Samizdat* contend that hunger for reliable news about the outer world and Russia itself has greatly increased the number of listeners to foreign Russian-language broadcasts; and this is supported by a certain amount of evidence of the BBC, Radio Free Europe, and Radio Vatican, who continue such broadcast programmes, jamming notwithstanding. It is reasonable, however, to conclude that Communist propaganda has the population of the Soviet Union efficiently 'sewn up'.

Communist operations in countries outside the Soviet orbit are naturally influenced by the existence of a hostile or an amenable political environment and by national characteristics; and where the Communist Parties have become familiar institutions, as in Italy and France, they acquire, chameleon-like, the colour of their surroundings. In these circumstances, as in the phenomenon of Euro-Communism, there is a certain tactical independence from Moscow even to the extent of criticising actions of the Soviet Government, such as the suppression of the 'dissidents'. But this does not alter the fact that Communist parties throughout the world with their fellow-travelling camp followers, except for those of the rival Chinese affiliation, are subordinate to the same central Soviet authority and normally respond to its imperatives. From 1920 to 1924 they operated more or less openly under the control of the Central Committee of the CPSU in Moscow which used the Comintern (Communist International) as its own secretariat, after which the Comintern had its offices in different countries. In 1943 it was officially dissolved. This was at the height of the war, when it was hoped to throw the mantle of Allied respectability over the Communist Resistance Movements which were, in fact, working, sometimes in co-operation with, but often in opposition to national resistance movements in every Nazi-occupied country. The aim of this exercise, which had only a partial and temporary success in places where the Red Army did not reach, was to entrench Communists in the government of the country when liberation came.

In 1947, when the tussle with the United States for the control of liberated Western Europe really began, the Cominform was set up, with headquarters at Belgrade (for Stalin had not yet broken with Tito) and a membership consisting of the CPSU, the Communist Parties of Eastern European countries already in the Soviet net, the French and Italian Parties. The Cominform was the means of orchestrating the 'Cold War' with the fanatical Zdhanov as conductor. It was dissolved in 1956.

Now it is the Central Committee of the CPSU, through its Secretariat and Apparatus, which controls and directs propaganda operations both at home and abroad. Several departments of the Central Committee are directly concerned in this work,[1] namely the Propaganda and International Departments and those for Foreign Cadres; Information; Socialist Countries; and the Political Administration of the Ministries of Defence. The Politburo itself, of which, among others Andropov the Chairman of the KGB is a member, certainly determines the principal themes and tactics of all external propaganda agencies at any given time. B.N. Ponomarev, now head of the International Department, has been involved for the past forty years in the international propaganda field, first in the Executive Committee of the Comintern, then as head of the Soviet office of the Cominform, then in various departments of the Central Committee.

Other old hands prominent in this field are K.V. Rusakov, now secretary in charge of relations with Socialist countries and M.V. Zimianiv, formerly Chief Editor of *Pravda*, now Secretary in charge of ideological questions. The Propaganda Department itself appears to be more concerned with internal than external activities (e.g. cultural enlightenment in various institutions; mass political work; Party propaganda and education; radio and television). The Foreign Cadres Department is concerned with Soviet personnel serving abroad (Ministry of Foreign Affairs; Ministry of Foreign Trade, etc.). The Information Department is responsible for the direction of TASS and, probably, in general, with information issued for foreign consumption. The International Department handles relations with Communist Parties in non-Communist countries; it consequently has the most scope for propaganda to advance Soviet policies, the co-ordination of a variety of front organisations, assistance to subversive movements (e.g. ETA, IRA); promotion of 'liberation' campaigns, and exploitation of anti-military groups etc. The Department has special divisons for Africa; Central Europe (meaning mainly Germany); Great Britain and the Commonwealth; Latin

America; the Near East; South-East Asia; Scandinavia and Iceland, and the United States. Every Embassy is, of course, fully briefed in the propaganda line of the moment and the KGB is involved in many of these operations. 'Dirty-tricks' departments are not lacking, including the 'Disinformation Bureau,' of which more anon. So much for the centrally controlled mechanism.

PARASITIC PROPAGANDA

Communist propaganda has been conducted during the years on a large scale and by an infinite variety of means. The most obvious of these are the direct emissions and publications of the Soviet authorities themselves, the broadcasts of the external radio services in fifty-three foreign languages, *TASS*, the news agency, which has had a striking expansion since the early 1960s, especially during the decolonisation of Africa, in which it now has offices in twenty-seven African capitals, and the outpouring of pamphlets, articles and pictures through the *Novosti* press agency and diplomatic missions. The open pronouncements of all the various Communist parties and of the Cuban and other satellite governments come into the same category.

Direct advocacies of the revolutionary theses or of Soviet policies or party statements are neither the main nor the most effective forms of propaganda, however. What distinguishes Communist propaganda as a whole from the missionary activity of any other political or religious institution in the world (the Catholic Church; or Islam; or Buddhism or nationalist doctines of any kind) is its essentially parasitic character. It is by fastening upon and battening upon existing group emotions, enthusiasms, idealisms, prejudices and especially sectional loyalties and hatreds, that it undermines the social integrity and unity of nations, confuses consciences and weakens the will to resist the strategy of the Soviet Union.

The enrolment of fellow-travellers, sympathisers and 'innocents' clubs', the natural outcome of foreign socialist and liberal sympathy with the Russian Revolution, has from the start been a means of extending the influence of the Party. But what has ever since improved the Communist technique of exploiting other groups and their enthusiasms for its own purpose was the adoption of the famous 'Trojan Horse' policy proposed by

Comrade Ercoli (alias Togliani the Italian Communist Party leader) at the 6th International Communist Congress. This technique of getting inside other bodies gave a great impetus to the proliferation of Front Organisations, which, started by Willi Muenzenberg, the leader of the German Party, fifty years ago, built up eventually to several thousand, some international, some regional, some confined to particular countries. George Dimitrov, Secretary-General of the Comintern at the time, expressed the underlying purposes very clearly:

Let our friends do the work. We must always remember that one sympathizer is generally worth more than a dozen Communists. A University Professor, who, without being a Party member, lends himself to the interests of the Soviet Union is worth more than a hundred men with Party cards. ... Our friends must confuse the adversary for us, carry out our main directions, influence in favour of our campaign people who do not think as we do, and whom we could never reach. Particularly we must use ambitious politicians who need support; men who realise that we Communists can clear a path for them, give them publicity and provide them with a ladder.

Such men will sell their souls to the Devil — and we buy souls.[2]

Many of the international Communist Front organisations, though they still exist, have had their day, partly because they have been bypassed by events, partly because their pretences to defend the interests of particular groups have been exposed and discredited, but there are some which have had more than a nuisance value. These include the World Peace Council; the World Federation of Trade Unions; the eleven Trade Union Internationals set up as rivals to the Trade Secretariats of the International Federation of Free Trade Unions; the International Organisation of Journalists; the International Radio and Television Organisation; the World Federation of Democratic Youth, with its biennial 'Youth Festivals' and the International Union of Students, whose fruits we all know. Front organisations for every kind of profession, but especially journalists, have blossomed in Latin America and in Africa throughout the decolonisation period — 'Pan African Union of Journalists', schools for journalists organised in Algeria, Mali, Guinea and East

Africa, etc. The anti-colonial front organisations had their heyday in Britain and Western Europe during the 1970s — and succeeded in penetrating the British Labour Party, in marked contrast to the Party's earlier exposure of the 'Communist Solar System'. They made inroads into the churches of those countries, and in the United States the 'American Committee on Africa', the principal Front Organisation, had great success in aligning pro-Black and anti-imperialist lobbies with the Communists' 'liberation' campaigns in Africa. Anti-apartheid is still a rallying cry on both sides of the Atlantic. It is probably the World Federation of Trade Unions that has been the most effective of these 'Fronts', by attracting influential Western trade unionists into the Soviet orbit and weakening the rival non-communist federation and its national components.

What however is more important than the mechanism of Communist propaganda is the progress that it has made in the last few years in penetrating and perverting the moral and spiritual codes of the historically Christian nations. This is particularly true in regard to the ethics of peace, war and revolution. There is evidence here of considerable theoretic study of these subjects and of the prevailing schools of thought about them by Communist intellectuals — editors of *Pravda*, for instance, who have taken full advantage of their contacts with their Catholic colleagues in UNESCO. The leftward trend of popular theologians and the local bureaucracies of the Church since the second Vatican Council, particularly in France, the Netherlands, Spain, Latin America and the United States has been assiduously cultivated; and it is by fastening upon and using, with the aid of Marxist priests, the emotional Catholic preoccupation with the Third World and the similar enthusiasms of the mainly Protestant World Council of Churches, that Communist propaganda has most successfully developed its parasitic technique.

It is with much the same allies that it is re-arousing the campaign against nuclear armaments which made its mark in the famous '*Ban-the-Bomb*' campaign of the 1950s. There is no question of the truth and the good that are to be found in each of these causes, the cause of justice for the indigenous peoples of South Africa, the fraternal obligation to aid the needy, and the cause of peace. It is by the unscrupulous exploitation of the emotions which these causes evoke among civilised people that the Communists have had no little success in serving the political aims of the Soviet Union, the projection of its power in Africa, Asia and Latin America and the weakening of its antagonists' military defences.

THE ANTI-COLONIAL LIBERATION CAMPAIGN

I need say no more about the Peace Campaign, since we have already noticed the extent to which the efforts of NATO to counter the current threat of the Soviets' strategic nuclear weapons in Western Europe are being impeded by the continuation of religious and Socialist opposition particularly in the Low Countries. It is in the anti-colonial 'liberation' campaigns that we have seen how far Communist propaganda can go in promoting passionate hatreds and spreading falsehoods on a vast scale through the complacent mass media of the Western world. It is a basic principle of Leninist doctrine (adapting the original Russian thesis of the 'struggle' of the workers and peasants against the aristocrats and the bourgeoisie to the 'struggle' of dependent peoples against their European rulers) that there is an inherent and radical hostility between the indigenous peoples of Africa, Asia and the Americas and the 'imperialists.'

Consequently Communists make war upon the ideal of a 'multi-racial society' in which Africans, Asians and Europeans coexist and co-operate with equal rights, and ideal which has been pursued *mutatis mutandis*, say, by the British in Kenya and Malaysia, the French in West Africa and the Portuguese in their particular colour-blind way in their great African dependencies. While anti-colonialism became the theme song of the United Nations, the Communists had great success by constant exaggeration, in stimulating racial hatred as a feature of progressive politics, until many churchmen of the West, in union with the Left, came to regard the coloured and especially Black races as the embodiment of injured virtue and the European and American 'capitalists' as the embodiment of unjust oppression.

The war in Vietnam showed how, thanks to the sensationalism of the mass media and especially American television, public opinion could be influenced by well-selected stories and pictures of the horrors of war and made to adopt sweeping judgments in favour of the Soviets' clients, the Vietminh, against both their indigenous South Vietnamese opponents and the United States forces. It was always the massive American bombings, never the continuous terrorism of the other side against the civilian population (the 'boat people' of a few years later) which received the publicity. The Vietnam war was indeed, for the United States, a deplorable miscarriage of intentions and a humiliating defeat, the traumatic effects of which have taken a long time to wear off. For the Communists it was an opportunity which they seized with both hands to entrench hostility to the Americans, and consequently to the Alliance which they lead, especially in the minds of the younger generation of several European countries.

No sooner was the Vietnam war over than the Soviet propaganda machine was turned at full blast upon the 'liberation' of Southern Africa. While successes had been gained here and there, often in rivalry with the Chinese, in some newly emancipated African states — Guinea, Tanzania, for instance, and, for a time, Zaire — and insurgency against Rhodesia and South West Africa was beginning to take shape, the Portuguese were still effectively ruling their African territories. Yet to secure the control of their two great provinces, Angola and Mozambique, was a necessary condition of any advance against South Africa, the last citadel of white rule in the continent. Despite a great deal of hopeful exaggeration about the prowess of the 'liberation armies', the disjointed insurgent activities which had continued since the first terrorist raid into Northern Angola in March 1961 took the Government of Dr Salazar by surprise, had really made very little progress against the increasingly efficient army, except that the small dependency of Guinea (Bissau), surrounded by hostile territory, was in a state of siege. This was largely due to the absence of any widespread discontent in the population of Angola and Mozambique, the intense efforts of the Caetano Government to expand education and improve social services, and the striking development of production, industry and trade, particularly in the former.

The leaders of the Portuguese regime, however, had failed to read the signs of the times, the pressure for democracy at home and the whole trend of international development. The army in Africa, more than half locally recruited, was never defeated and held its own remarkably well[3] until paralysed by the collapse of the metropolitan authority in the Lisbon Revolution of April

1974, the climax of nine years of well-organised conspiracy by the Portuguese Communist Party. In the last five years particularly, every device had been used by the Communists to whip up feeling against the Portuguese. In Britain and the United States, particularly among the heirs of the Non-Conformist Conscience, the *nigra legenda* was in full swing. All the old moral indignation of the anti-slavery campaign of a century ago was revived and the maximum Anglo-Saxon prejudice against a Latin nation was aroused. Hardly less obsolete and quite inaccurate accusations of Portuguese forced labour were fed to Left-wing and Catholic news agencies and papers all over Europe. Bit by bit the British Labour Party and the other Social Democratic parties of Europe were induced to endorse the various anti-colonial Communist Front organisations.

DISINFORMATION

In the prevailing atmosphere of bias it was easy to sell any fabricated tale of Portuguese villainy to credulous newspaper editors and producers of television programmes. It is here that the Disinformation Bureau of the KGB in Prague came into use. Its main activity is to plant forgeries and inaccurate reports in the Press of countries outside the Soviet orbit. Between 1957 and 1970 the Intelligence Services of the Western Powers uncovered thirty-two 'plants' of this kind, chiefly designed to foster anti-American feeling. In addition to providing 'revelations' through published letters falsely attributed to Ministers and other misrepresentations of government positions, the Bureau has been busy discrediting non-Communist trade unions in the course of the campaign to promote the Communist domination of the trade union movement, particularly in Africa.

The contribution of the Bureau to the anti-Portuguese campaign was the famous case of Wyriamu. This unidentifiable, and in fact non-existent village, said to be in the Tete Province of Mozambique, was selected for the narration of an horrific massacre attributed to Portuguese commandos. There were recognisable features of torture, women and men separated for purposes of mass execution and the heads of decapitated civilians used as footballs, which are familiar to students of the Communist atrocity vocabulary. This horror story was first planted in an obscure Italian Communist newspaper where it attracted little publicity. Then came urgent orders to whip up feeling in Britain so as to spoil the visit of the Portuguese Prime Minister to London in July 1973 for celebrations of the 700th anniversary of the Anglo — Portuguese Alliance.

The scheme worked perfectly. An English Marxist priest (who had never been to Mozambique) succeeded in persuading the Editor of *The Times* to publish the report a day or two before Dr Caetano's visit. It was taken up in no time by the BBC. Questions were asked in Parliament; virtuous condemnations appeared in many newspapers; correspondents hurried to Mozambique to investigate. In the end no-one could find any village of that name or any witness to corroborate the story. The Portuguese Army authorities, traduced as a matter of course by foreign commentators but in fact no less jealous of discipline than the British military in Ulster, conducted an enquiry which found no evidence to confirm it. The priest went to and fro for some weeks professing to substantiate his story with the help of some expelled Spanish missionaries of his own poltical persuasion. Wyriamu soon disappeared from the news; but not before a legend had been created. It became part of the martyrology of the Left; and in the summer of 1979 when Samora Machel, now President of Mozambique, published in his official bulletin a long diatribe against the Catholic Church, in answer to protests at his arbitrary expulsion of clergy, he accused the Bishops of being still identified with the Portuguese imperialists who were responsible, among other malpractices, for 'Wyriamu'.'

What ventures of Communist propaganda are we to expect in the years to come? Black nationalist insurgency in South Africa is bound to provide a certain amount of activity. Now that 'Liberation' has been temporarily tamed by the Zimbabwe settlement, however, the prospects of 'bleeding heart' campaigns in the Western world do not look very promising. It seems probable to me that, at a time when the choice between better — and more costly — defence against the Soviet colossus or a policy of compromise with it has become the major prolem of all the Western democracies, it is rather in exploiting the Campaign for Nuclear Disarmament that we shall find the expertise of Communist propaganda employed in the immediate future.

Part Three

Developments of the North Atlantic Alliance

11 The problem of unity amid diversity

Prophecy, as I suggested at the beginning of this book, is an unprofitable exercise. But there is one conditional forecast which can be made with assurance. It is that, if political divisions between the signatories of the North Atlantic Treaty become so serious that their co-operation to resist aggression against any one of them cannot be depended upon, the CPSU will certainly use its military superiority to achieve the domination of Europe. Whether this were done by open war on the German front, or by using a local situation elsewhere as a pretext for intervention, or by the process of blackmail which Lord Hill-Norton foresees,[1] the President of the United States would be faced with an appalling quandary. Should he risk a nuclear war with the real danger of escalation to intercontinental proportions, or acquiesce in some formula of European neutralisation which would amount to capitulation and the dissolution of the Atlantic Alliance?

The political situation, envisaged by Brigadier Shelford Bidwell and his colleagues in their *World War 3*[2] as the setting for the outbreak of hostilities, though very different from the speculation of General Hackett and his collaborators in their *Third World War*,[3] is by no means impossible.

Taking account of the opportunities for 'crisis management', which a commitment to *détente* and the Helsinki Conference formulas for Security and Co-operation in Europe offered to a British Labour Government, 'the usual uneasy alliance of power-ful Left-wingers and timid moderates', an American President immersed in domestic politics and a French Government temporally estranged from its German partners, these authors find them tangled in 'hot wires' to Moscow in embarrassed efforts to avoid military resistance to a Soviet 'police action' against West Germany. In consequence, the Bundswehr is left to bear the brunt of the Warsaw Pact invasion until the British, American,

115

French and other Allied forces are tardily compelled to defend themselves. The imagined cause of the Soviet attempt to attack Germany in isolation from its American and European allies and so avoid involving outright war between NATO and the Warsaw Pact — a secret German base for producing nuclear weapons — is fortunately very wide of the mark. For nothing is further from the policy of the Federal Government than to make Germany, in defiance of the Treaty of Brussels, a nuclear power (as witness Helmut Schmidt's refusal to accept the 'double-key' system for the modernised American 'theatre nuclear missiles' which the North Atlantic Council decided in December 1979 to station on German territory). But the inadequacy of the defence budgets of the European Allies before 1977 and the American mood of appeasement which accompanied the long-drawn SALT II negotiations created a depressing sense of NATO's weakness which given credibility to Brigadier Bidwell's picture of the disarray of the West when the Soviets decide to strike.

On the other hand, the turn of the tide, in the matter of military preparedness and political support for the Atlantic Alliance, which General Hackett discerned at the end of the 1970s accounts for the more reassuring picture of united allied reaction to the imagined Soviet offensive which his book offers to its readers. But, however, we may speculate upon the political conditions which might influence the Soviets' decision to risk, or not to risk, war in pursuit of their European objective, one thing is indisputable. It is that the outcome of the duel of wills and arms, when and if it comes, will be primarily determined by the unity or disunity of the Atlantic Allies. How then do they stand in relation to one another and to the Alliance itself in 1980?

The political and military mechanism of NATO at Evere and Mons in Belgium seemed to be working efficiently. That in itself is an important asset; and, though on a much smaller scale than the relentless Soviet armament programme, the strengthening of its land, naval and air forces and those of the French was making real progress both in quantity and quality. On the other hand, the distinctive positions which we saw the Allied governments adopt at the end of 1979, in regard both to meeting the Soviet nuclear threat in the European theatre and to the Afghanistan question, revealed real national differences which show no signs of diminishing. The most serious question, of course, is the cohesion of the American and European parts of the Alliance. It

is not only a question of the credibility of the nuclear umbrella of
the United States, which we have already discussed, but of the
extent to which there is, or is not in the minds of the American
people and their European allies a common purpose to deter and
resist the aggressive expansion of Soviet power by whatever means
are needed.

THE UNITED STATES POSITION

In this respect much the most convincing evidence of American
commitment to the common purpose is the presence in Europe,
despite the vagaries of Congressional moods and White House
diplomacy, of quite considerable United States conventional
forces. Not long ago Senator Manfield's demand to 'bring the
boys home' expressed a powerful wave of feeling, and the
Jackson — Nunn Amendment to the 1974 Defence Appropriations
Act actually instructed the President to begin reducing US forces
in Europe in the following year by the percentage of the deficit in
the Balance of Payments due from European allies for the cost of
stationing them there. The fact that we hear nothing nowadays of
these pettyfogging shop-keeping arguments is a measure of the
change which has occurred. It is not, I think, due so much to a
better appreciation of the European contribution to the
manpower and costs of NATO, though the State Department
laboured valiantly in Dr Kissinger's day to educate public opinion
on that subject, as to a better understanding of the Soviet Union's
hostile challenge to America. For, while every variation of
attitude to the Soviets which can be discovered in Western
European countries, from pacifism and a belief in Marxism to the
most fervent and bellicose hostility to Communism, can be found
in the United States, it is a distinguishing characteristic of
Americans — an intensely patriotic people — that they see the
drama of the world as a bilateral drama played out between
'God's own country' and the rival super power. So long as there
was a hope of winning the co-operation of the latter in moving
towards their ideal of peace and stability, *détente* appealed to the
ineradicable optimism of the Americans. But the successive blows
which the Soviets have inflicted upon this hopefulness (Cubans in
Angola and Ethiopia; flouting of the 'human rights' campaign;
the threat to the energy resources of the Middle East; Afghanistan)
have hardened their hearts and confirmed the view of world

affairs as essentially a duel between the United States and the Soviet Union. Europe is the main arena of contest between the two. But it is not as a favour to Germany, Britain, France, Italy or the lesser allies that American forces, land, sea and air, are in Europe. It is mainly — and quite rightly as I see it — for the national defence of the United States. So here are 202 400 United States soldiers deployed on this side of the Atlantic Ocean and 74 300 of the US Air Force, as well as the 6th Fleet in the Mediterranean. It is hardly possible that any military or naval thrust of the Soviets would not collide with these American forces, precipitate fighting and bring the North Atlantic Treaty into play. That is the great trip-wire; it is a commitment to Article 5 of the treaty more immediate and convincing than the problematical resort to nuclear arms.

Governments and people in most European allied countries habitually rely on that commitment. But that does not prevent a variety of national reactions to the shifting attitudes of the American President in regard to the Soviet Union.

The quick change of President Jimmy Carter from his belief in *détente* and arms control to his bellicose response to the Soviet occupation of Afghanistan, disturbed the cautious as well as the Russophil elements in Western Europe, just as it warmed the hearts of those most alive to the Soviet threat. But it also left a wide-spread impression of diplomatic ineptitude which has not strengthened respect for American leadership in the non-Communist world. The almost complete paralysis of the United States Intelligence Services, resulting from Congressional reaction to the Nixon era, and the consequent failure of the CIA to foresee any of the recent dramatic happenings (Ethiopia; Iran; Afghanistan) has also contributed to the decline of confidence in Washington. Much as they deplored, as had the General Assembly of the United Nations, the Soviet Government's military occupation of Afghanistan, there were few governments therefore which concurred in President Carter's proposals to punish the Soviet Union with sanctions which former Presidents had never invoked after the no less flagrant military interventions in Czechoslovakia in 1968 and Angola in 1976. In the United States Mr Reagan's election to the Presidency and the Republicans' success in the senatorial elections of 1980 aired not a little to dissatisfaction with the vacillating foreign policy of the Carter Administration.

THE BRITISH POSITION

Mrs Thatcher's government in the United Kingdom was alone in giving unqualified support to the United States. Alliance with the Americans is more of an ingrained habit with the British, and especially the Conservatives, than it is with other Europeans.

NATO has until recently been outside party politics in the Britain. The Atlantic Treaty was the work of a Labour government which the Conservative and Liberal parties of the day warmly endorsed. In 1980, however, there was a perceptible danger of it becoming a party issue, not indeed because of any spontaneous movement of public opinion, but because of the progress made by the militant Left in capturing the machinery of the Labour Party and the violent hostility of the Trade Union leaders to the Thatcher Government. The Government's policy of increasing defence expenditure in order to strengthen NATO caused it to welcome the American President's return to a more virile policy towards Moscow. The historic experience of the British in defending the Persian Gulf and its oil wells, and of resisting Russian pressure on Afghanistan throughout the days of the *Raj* in India, made the British government particularly sensitive to the threat of a southward move by the Soviets in that directions. Except for a recurrence of the age-old Francophobia, stimulated by disputes over Britain's financied contributions to the European Economic Community, British relations with its other Atlantic allies in Canada and Europe are no less cordial.

THE FRENCH POSITION

Very different is the position of France. For both the Americans' handling of the proposed nuclear defence of the European theatre and their attempt at the beginning of 1980 to secure their allies' co-operation in strong measures against Moscow because of the Afghanistan affair revived the French refusal to be treated, in the words of President Giscard d'Estaing, as a 'province' of the United States. He took the occasion of a broadcast to the nation to define the distinctive, independent position of France and followed this with a prolonged visit to the Gulf States, Saudi Arabia and Jordan, which did much to strengthen French friendship and commerce with the Arab world as well as securing supplies of Abu

Dhabi and Kuwait oil. That is only one aspect of a vigorous foreign policy which displays, among other things, a far-greater readiness than any of its allies to intervene, when asked, to resist Communist-inspired mischief in African countries, as did French paratroopers with great effect in Zaire in 1978.

In fact France maintains a distinctive position in relation to the United States, her European allies, her former colonies, Soviet Russia, China and the 'unaligned' countries. It is not merely the legacy of Charles de Gaulle's revolt against what he considered to be American pretensions in the 1960s, though the particular attitude of detachment from the integrated command structure of NATO while remaining a member of the Atlantic Alliance was his own formula. It is the characteristic of an old and proud nation, which has never in history been a subordinate member of a coalition and is in many ways more 'insular' than the English, after the humiliation which it suffered in the Second World War. France is an effective member of various international organisation — the United Nations (UNESCO's headquarters are in Paris), the European Community, OECD, the Atlantic Alliance and the Western European Union and is a party to many bilateral treaties, but always on a basis of equality.

In particular, the French Government — and on this all political parties, Left, Right and Centre are united — clings to the traditional right of a sovereign state to organise its own defence independently, though this does not, of course mean that it pursues its strategic planning, arms procurement and communications organisation *in vacuo*. Though the defence of the national territory is the first consideration, co-operation with allies in the event of war is prepared, particularly at sea. France is now the third nuclear power in the world; and it is British rather than French unwillingness that accounts for the absence of co-operation between the two European nuclear powers. The French defence budget has increased each year for the past five years.

Surtout pas trop de zèle is the French attitude to the Atlantic Alliance. There is no reason to doubt France's commitment to Article 5 of the North Atlantic Treaty, but she will do all that is possible to prevent the need for it. Her attachment to *détente* is, the French would say, the logical consequence. But there is more to it than that: for Franco-Russian friendship is a very old vintage; it dates back to the origins of the Dual Alliance in 1893. Though the French Government, like all the Atlantic Allies and

Japan, is a party to COCOM, whose business is to prevent the export to Communist states of material or inventions of military utility, it sees every advantage in keeping up trade and investment and — so far as it does not offend its own very vocal critics of the Soviets' repression of dissidents — cultural relations with the Soviet Union and the Socialist states of Eastern Europe. This also has the advantage of keeping the French Communist Party quiet.

This explains the French refusal to engage in anything like a crusade led by the United States against the Soviet Union, whether over Afghanistan, the Olympic boycott, or anything else. It is a tragedy that Britain's belated membership of the European Common Market should have led to a temporary poisoning of Anglo — French relations with quarrels about money, fish and 'sheep-meat' which lead to outbursts of Anglophobia and Francophobia by farmers, fishermen and tradesmen on both sides of the Channel. Fortunately this does not affect the basic friendship of intelligent people in the two countries. More important in regard to essential strategy is the Franco-German treaty, which was General de Gaulle's greatest contribution to European unity. We shall see the value of this when considering the German position in the Alliance.

THE ITALIAN POSITION

Italy, though not lacking internal problems aplenty, is not troubled with grievances against any of its allies. Italian relations with the United States, to which millions of Italians have emigrated, are traditionally good. Italy, whose financial position is not brilliant, has much in common with the United Kingdom in the EEC but is on good terms with Germany — which has at times come to its aid with massive loans on favourable terms — with France and its other colleagues. The recurrent parliamentary crises have not so far impaired the efficiency of the armed forces, of which the modernised navy is particularly valuable to NATO. The Communist Party, which remains the second largest in the country and a kind of national institution, is of the Euro-Communist variety and (for whatever reason) does not oppose Italy's membership of the Atlantic Alliance. Indeed Italy agreed like the United Kingdom to have cruise missiles situated on its territory as part of the new European nuclear defence system of the Alliance. Naples is the headquarters of the Southern European Command of NATO, as well as the principal port of the United States 6th Fleet. The staff college of NATO is in Rome.

THE GERMAN POSITION

The position of the German Federal Republic is of central importance, both politically and militarily, to the viability of the Atlantic Alliance. It is divided numerically almost equally between the Social Democrat Party and its Liberal allies and the Christian Democrats with its Bavarian Christian Social allies; but, though the latter, while in opposition, have put more emphasis on defence against the Soviets than on conciliating them, they are basically united in foreign policy. From the very creation of the Federal Republic in the zones of the country which had remained under the occupation of the Western Powers after the defeat of Hitler, it had relied for its defence upon the military power of the United States. Today the situation is not so simple. There is no question of Federal Germany's attachment to the American alliance as essential to its security, or of its devotion to the ideal of the democratic society, which it shares with the United States; but, while the original nuclear supremacy of the Americans has been transformed into a position which is, at best, equivalent to that of the Soviets, a great concentration of the latter's conventional military power, far greater than the combined strength of the Atlantic Alliance, confronts Germany along the whole of its land frontier.

The Federal Republic's army and air force are far the largest contribution, in terms of manpower, to the strength of NATO. Consequently there is nowadays more of an equal partnership between Washington and Bonn than there is between any other pair of allies; and the US government is bound — difficult as it is — to take account of the peculiar problems and policies of the German Federal government in regard to its Eastern neighbours — the sundered part of Germany itself, the 'German Democratic Republic' which has Berlin for the its capital — the Soviet Union, Poland and Czechoslovakia. The *Ostpolitik* whereby Willy Brandt, when Chancellor; contrived to 'normalise' so far as possible diplomatic relations, trade and communications with those countries, has always been difficult to reconcile with NATO security: but it has brought such tangible benefits to the German people that no government would willingly jeopardise it. The reconciliation with Poland, symbolised by the German Chancellor weeping as he knelt on his visit to the former concentration camp at Auschwitz, to atone for the crimes of Nazi Germany, is a moral gain on either side, and the freedom for Germans living in Poland to return to the Fatherland, which he negotiated, was most popular. *Détente* is for most countries no more than a political formula, devoid of human impact, but for the many thousand Berliners and West Germans who have been enabled to visit their families in the 'Democratic Republic' the advantages of the agreements made in 1971 are very real. That is why it was politically impossible for Helmut Schmidt to risk widening the rift with the East by endorsing President Carter's proposals for drastic action against the Soviet Union because of its occupation of Afghanistan.

This tussle between *détente* and firmness in defence was typical of the dilemma which is bound to remain with any German Government in the foreseeable future. It is a problem which confronts *mutatis mutandis* both French and German Governments in view of their different political histories. Herr Helmut Schmidt, who was in Paris in February 1980 for one of the regular ministerial meetings in accordance with the Franco-German Treaty, took the opportunity to make a joint declaration with President Giscard d'Estaing on the Afghanistan question which was firm but very moderate in tone. It may be taken as representative of the position of the European allies of the United States other than the British. The meeting also gave the two statesmen the opportunity to confirm their military alliance.

THE OTHER ALLIES IN WESTERN EUROPE

Different as are the domestic politics of the other Atlantic Allies in Western Europe — Norway, Denmark, the Netherlands, Belgium, Luxembourg, Portugal and Iceland — they have no particular causes of difference or friction with the United States, Canada, Britain, France, Germany, Italy or one another, except for the intermittent 'cod war' of Iceland with the British and

Germans, now happily in abeyance. I have already drawn attention to the endemic weakness in the northern countries caused by the Socialist hankering for appeasement with the Soviet Union, which is in marked contrast to the way in which German Social Democrats in government have combined the inevitable concessions to the *Ostpolitik* with the maintenance of the most formidable conventional forces in the Atlantic Alliance. There are recurrent movements in both the Netherlands and Belgium for the reduction of military service or of the national contribution to NATO, due in the former to Christian pacifist tendencies, in the latter to the undying and bitter feud between Flemings and Walloons. In both countries the governments, with sufficient public support, have kept up their commitments to the North Atlantic Council. The Communist Parties in Portugal and Iceland, both of which have been at intervals represented in government, are, of course, hostile to the Atlantic Alliance as a whole and the United States in particular. In 1980, however, they were in both cases in opposition. Though the Portuguese Government, which has since the 1979 election been in Centre-Right hands, toys with the 'unaligned group' in order to keep on good terms with Angola and Mozambique, if only to secure a better deal for the Portuguese citizens remaining in those Communist states, it takes seriously its contribution to the European Command of NATO, for which a brigade has been trained with German and Canadian help, as well as the part which it had always played in the Atlantic Command. It also offered the use of the air base on Terceira in the Azores to the United States, if required as a staging post for flights to the Middle East in the Afghanistan crisis. The present Icelandic Government has dropped the idea of asking the United States to withdraw from Keflavik, the air base which is of such vital importance for naval strategy in the North Atlantic.

NATIONAL ANTIPATHIES IN THE SOUTH-EAST

An entirely different situation, which is a serious impediment to the military capacity of the Alliance as a whole, exists in the south-eastern part of the Treaty Area, owing to the latest stage of the secular feud between Greece and Turkey. The armed forces of the two countries had, since their adherence to the North

Atlantic Treaty in 1950, been under the command of the American Commander-in-Chief of the southern sector, with headquarters at Ismir in Turkey. American aid to both countries involved the creation of a number of US bases in each, including advanced radar reconnaissance posts in Anatolia, and the use of their harbours, particularly the Piraeus, by the United States 6th Fleet. The whole of this co-operative complex of defence was dislocated since the Greeks, in protest at the Turkish invasion of Cyprus in 1974, withdraw their forces from the integrated command of NATO — which involved pulling their officers out of Ismir — and threatened to put an end to all military facilities for the United States on Greek territory. Prospecting for oil in the Aegean sea-bed became another bone of contention between Greece and Turkey, and the Greeks refused to allow any aircraft to fly to or from Turkey through their air space above the Aegean Sea. Meanwhile bad feeling was caused against the United States in Turkey, because Congress in Washington insisted upon holding up the supply of promised military material, on the grounds that the Turkish army in Cyprus had used arms provided by the United States.

There was thus a serious danger of Turkey turning towards Moscow. By March 1980 this cat's cradle of troubles was in process of disentanglement thanks to the diplomacy of the State Department and persistent efforts at conciliation by the civil and military authorities of NATO. By the end of 1980 agreement had been reached and the Greek forces were reintegrated in the Command Structure of the Alliance. At the same time negotiations for the admission of Greece to the European Economic Community were completed. In Turkey the Army had once again stepped in, established a military government to replace the feuds of the politicians and cope with the terrorism of extremists. Good relations were re-established with the United States, Turkey was still in a state of acute economic crisis, from which the German Federal Government, anxious to remedy this weakness in the structure of the alliance, was determined to rescue it with substantial financial aid. I shall return in a later chapter to the strategic problem of this southern flank of NATO. The situation between the two Allies concerned has certainly improved in the last year; but there is no sign of an acceptable settlement in Cyprus, which is the fount and origin of the trouble.

However real and insoluble the differences in temperament,

tradition and interest of these fifteen allied states, there is no doubt that opposition to any kind of alien Communist domination unites the bulk of their peoples. Fear is a powerful cement.

12 Nuclear arms and policies

The military tasks which the defence forces of the Atlantic Alliance must prepare to discharge are so varied in their nature and their geographical setting that I propose to study them under five heads; first, in this chapter, the place of nuclear weapons in the Western armoury; then, the Northern Theatre of Operations; next the Central-German Front; then the Southern Theatre, and, lastly, the tasks of the Allied Navies with in and beyond the Treaty Area.

There is a fundamental political difference between the attitude of the United States, their allies and the non-Communist peoples in general to the whole question of using nuclear weapons of mass destruction and the attitude of the CPSU. To the former it is a matter of conscience; to the latter, not. To the former, who are directly or indirectly heirs of the Christian civilisation and its humane derivations, there is an ingrained repugnance to the wholesale killing of human beings, even in the exercise of a nation's natural right of self-defence. The danger of an enemy inflicting such a holocaust upon our own society does not, for many, annul this repugnance, which found its most forthright expression in the declaration of the second Vatican Council (1963–5) that: 'Any act of war aimed indiscriminately at the destruction of entire cities or of extensive areas with their population is a crime against God and man himself and merits unequivocal and unhesitating condemnation.'[1]

The unescapable requirements of defence against a power which recognises no superior criterion of conduct, human or divine, compel the governments of other states to be ready to repel force with equivalent force. Yet we find throughout the history of nuclear arms from 1945 to today a persistent, though largely ineffective, effort to limit and then reduce them, to prevent their proliferation, restrict the testing of them, etc. We have already noticed the recurrence of anti-nuclear and disarmament movements in several of the NATO countries and the deeply rooted hope of the Americans of finding in their Communist adversaries some common desire for peace and stability. And the basis of all this reaction of the civilised conscience, in this second half of the twentieth century, to the weapons of mass destruction is, simply, respect for the value of human life.

That basis is entirely lacking in the minds of the Soviet leaders. Their own morality, as Lenin[2] taught, 'is entirely subordinated to the interests of the proletariat and the needs of the class struggle', as they understand it, and the cause of the World Revolution.

The merit of any course of action, whether of war or peace, is judged solely by its practical use at any given time to advance that cause, with which their own Russian ambitions are identified; and there is no moral distinction between any military devices or types of weapon, conventional, nuclear, chemical or biological. They will avoid inter-state war so long as 'peaceful coexistence' — in which arms-control palavers with their rivals have their part to play — advances the 'correlation of forces' to their advantage. They are unlikely to precipitate war unless they can see the quasi-certanty of success. But they must be ready at any time to fight and win, which involves the accumulation of the most modern and powerful armaments, including, in particular, inter-continental nuclear missiles designed to destroy those of their opponents in a 'first strike' and the means to survive 'second strike' retaliation. We have seen in earlier chapters the nature of the strategy and current tactics of the CPSU in which such American and NATO concepts as 'deterrence', 'flexible response', 'escalation' and 'mutual assured destruction' have no place, and something of the quantity and quality of their own nuclear and conventional arms.

I have put first the ethical principle or prejudice[3] concerning the indiscriminate destructive power of nuclear explosives, because it is something of which every democratic government is obliged to take account — a fact which itself inevitably tilts the strategic balance in favour of the Soviet Union.

No annual defence plans or estimates can be debated in any parliament (as in the two days' debate on the 1980 Defence Estimates in the British House of Commons) without speeches or motions giving expression to it. Hostility to Britain's 'nuclear deterrent' has become a permanent feature among a growing minority within the Labour Party. In the Netherlands a million signatories were obtained in a few weeks for a petition, organised with the help of the clergy, against the proposed introduction of the 'Neutron bomb'. In December 1979 the fall of the Van Agt coalition Government was only averted when the Premier promised to insist upon proposals for the mutual elimination of theatre nuclear weapons being made to the Soviet Union as a condition of abstaining from a vote against the North Atlantic Council's decision to station the new weapons in Europe. Owing to similar pressure in Belgium, no agreement to station these nuclear weapons in that country has as yet been made with the government in Brussels.

All this is, of course, a consummate nuisance to the defence planners of NATO and to the considerable technical community necessarily concerned with research and development of the new and more effective armaments which the sea, land and air forces of the Allies require. Because of it, however, the whole political approach of the Americans and their allies to the nuclear duel with the Russians has been overlaid for nearly twenty years with the notion of 'arms control'. Thus at present, in the early 1980s, SALT II is the cumulative result of years of bilateral conversations between the Soviet Union and the United States about the mutual limitation of their intercontinental thermo-nuclear ballistic missiles. It complicates not only the American task of maintaining, protecting and improving their own arsenal — about which there is a running fight in Washington between the Arms Control Lobby and the Pentagon — but also the nuclear defence of their European allies. For, except for the freedom from this ethico-political tangle which the French enjoy, and for the British naval and air contributions to NATO's nuclear potential, the whole of the nuclear defence in the European theatre of operations depends upon the United States, either by the 'dual-key' system under which no tactical nuclear weapons can be used without a positive decision of the President of the United States or through the direct responsibility of American personnel in the case of the proposed IRBMs and cruise missiles.

SALT II

The prolonged deferment of ratification of the SALT II Treaty by the United States, in reaction to Soviet behaviour in 1979–80, made the future of arms-control a more than ever elusive subject. Europeans are in two minds about the possible extension of the bilateral bargain between the two super powers, which the SALT Treaty now is, to cover their own defences. One school of thought, most evident among the Social Democrats of the German Federal Republic and their allied neighbours in Northern Europe, would like to see a SALT III which included both the Atlantic Alliance's nuclear defence of the European theatre and the Soviet IRBMs aimed at European targets, with a view to the reduction and ultimate withdrawal of both.

This attitude eventually prevailed in the North Atlantic Council. At its critical meeting in December 1979 when it was resolved to base 108 of the Pershing 2 missile launchers and 464 of the cruise missiles under American control in European allied countries to counter the threat of the Soviet Union's Backfire bombers and their SS4, SS5 and mobile SS20 IRBMs, the Council made a definite offer to the Soviet government. It offered to negotiate the reduction of the theatre nuclear forces — which would be installed in 1983 — as well as the intercontinental missiles with which SALT II is concerned. It announced the unilateral withdrawal of 1000 American tactical nuclear warheads from Europe (out of a total of about 7000) and this has already taken place. It proposed an interim agreement to give an impetus to the stalled MBFR negotiations at Vienna, and declared its readiness to consider a disarmament conference in Europe. The United States Government followed this up with an invitation to the Soviet Union to begin negotiations on limiting European theatre nuclear forces. The Soviet response to those advances at first was negative. At a meeting of the Warsaw Pact Leaders in May 1980, however, the Soviets renewed a proposal to 'freeze' the development of the SS20 missiles, whatever that may mean, if NATO agreed to do the same. (This would simply mean perpetuating the existing imbalance, since the Soviets already had some 150 SS20s deployed.)

The contrary attitude to the extension of the SALT Treaty, which is particularly manifest among those directly concerned with their national defences, is one of opposition to any interference with their country's freedom to develop its own armaments, in association with its allies, by submitting to restrictions negotiated by the United States and the CPSU. From this point of view, the chief objections are to certain articles of the SALT II Treaty itself, particularly its 'non-circumvention' clause and to the protocol attached to it — if and when the US Senate approves ratification of them; and also to the prospect that the limitations contained in the protocol could be embodied in a third step of the Strategic Arms Limitation Talks (SALT III) to which the European Allies might be constrained to adhere. France, whose independent nuclear *force de frappe* is now well developed, declines any part in the debate.

At this point we must look at what SALT II and its protocol involve. The Treaty, which was to last until 1985, gives form to the bargain struck by Presidents Ford and Brezhnev at Vladivostok in 1975 with certain modifications. A total of 2400 strategic delivery vehicles of intercontinental nuclear missiles, land-based and launched from submarines, is to be available to each signatory, but with an understanding that they are to be reduced by agreement to a figure between 2160 and 2260 during the term of the Treaty. There is a sub-limit of 1320 land- and submarine-launched missiles armed with multiple re-entry warheads (MIRV) and aircraft equipped with long-range cruise missiles. There are also a number of detailed provisions. To suggest, as some politicians are tempted to do, that this codified stalemate of over-kill capacities, has any relation to disarmament is, of course, nonsense, because any one of the warheads carried by more than 4800 or more of these intercontinental missiles could destroy human life in an area much greater than Hiroshima; and they are cumulatively far more lethal than the weapons possessed by the two super-powers when these talks started in 1964. All that can be said for SALT is that it freezes for five years the 'essential equivalence' in the maximum number of intercontinental missiles on either side with the possibility of a slight reduction. The 'non-circumvention' clause, to which the Soviet government attaches great importance, excludes the possibility of transferring any new nuclear weapons or devices to third parties, that is, to the NATO allies of the United States, and presumably, to the Cubans and East Germans on the other side. The Americans, however, claim that this does not preclude their continuing to supply nuclear material, under existing agreements, to their allies, that is to say essential parts of the Polaris system to the British. It is very likely that the Soviet Union would object to the replacement of this system by a new one, such as the Trident. An even more trouble-some provision is the restriction against supplying cruise missiles to a third party. For the cruise missile has many advantages, in cost, accuracy and mobility, as against the ballistic missile, notably for the medium-sized powers and for operation in a particular theatre of operations, which is why, even before SALT II is ratified, the cruise missiles have been adopted by NATO as the principal counterpart of the Soviet Union's nuclear threat to Western Europe. Because of the SALT restrictions these cruise missiles will have to be airborne and to remain in American ownership.

When the Treaty was signed, the protocol was planned to last only until September 1981; it will clearly have to be prolonged if it is to survive at all. It imposes limitations more clearly dis-advantageous to the American side than to the Soviets'. It bans the deployment of mobile ICBM launchers (which, as we shall see, is one of the options proposed as a remedy for the vulner-ability of the fixed American missiles sites) and flight testing from such launchers; it restricts the flight testing and deployment of new types of ballistic missiles; and it bans the testing and deploy-ment of airborne cruise missiles with a range exceeding 2500 km and of cruise missiles launched from land, surface vessels or submarines, capable of flying more than 600 km. What many European defence experts, as well as critics of the Treaty in the United States foresee is pressure on the President, both by the Soviet government and the Arms Control Lobby at home, to agree to prolong the life of the protocol and then include its restrictions in a future SALT III Treaty.

The actual number of intercontinental ballistic missiles, according to the published figures[4] at present available to the Soviet Union is 1398 ICBMs and 1028 SLBMs, total 2426; and to the USA 1054 ICBMs and 656 SLBMs; the American missiles, however, have many more warheads than those of the Soviet Union. To these must be added the sixty-four SLBMs of the four British Polaris submarines, making a total for NATO of 1674. If the French, in the event of war, were to employ their nuclear arm in fulfilling their treaty obligations, there would also be the eighty M20 missiles of their five nuclear submarines, and their eighteen land-based IRBMs.

VULNERABILITY OF AMERICAN LAND-BASED MISSILES

That is the position in regard to the Strategic Nuclear Arms which NATO regards as the ultimate stage of its defences, if neither conventional forces nor tactical nuclear weapons sufficed to contain and defeat an offensive by the Warsaw Pact. In the curious vocabulary peculiar to the moralistic policies of the West, not only the readiness to use these missiles, but the missiles themselves have come to be called 'the deterrent'. Before looking at the future of the even more oddly named 'British Independent Deterrent', we must consider the practical value of the United States strategic arms which constitute the bulk of the Western Alliance's nuclear potential.

There can be no doubt that the American superiority in these weapons, which popular opinion has so long taken for granted, is now no more; and it is the will-o'-the-wisp of *détente* which is the main cause. As a wide-awake American report puts it:

> Since the late 1960s, the United States has attempted to use restraint and arms limitation as the preferred means of maintaining strategic stability. It has not been successful in this effort. ... Stability is not being promoted by SALT or by continued U.S. restraint; it is being eroded by determined Soviet action and relative U.S. inaction.[5]

The chief defect in the American strategic arms systems, for which remedies are now being attempted, is the vulnerability of the 1000 Minuteman missiles in their fixed silos, which enemy reconnaissance satellites, of course, pinpoint. The US Secretary of Defense, Harold Brown, in his Department of Defense Annual Report, Fiscal Year 1980, writes: 'At some point in the early to mid 1980s, the Soviets, with a first strike, could eliminate the bulk of our ICBM silos and still retain a large number of warheads in reserve.' The reason for this forecast is, not only the increased throw-weight and accuracy of the Soviets' new ICBMs, but their known strategy of making their opponents' fixed missile sites, naval, military and air command posts and key industrial centres their prime targets, rather than the mass destruction of cities, which the Americans, with their unreciprocated doctrine of Mutual Assured Destruction (MAD), have in view — as also (it must be admitted) have the British Polaris missiles. What is being done to remedy this situation is, first, to increase the number and fire-power of the submarine ballistic missile force, and secondly, to make the land-based missile as mobile as possible. As for the first, the latest Trident submarines will have the size, capability and range of over 4000 miles equal to the Delta II monsters of the Soviet navy, which lying off the Kola Peninsula or the Northern coast of Norway could hit any target in North America or China. These huge nuclear submarines, however, despite all the latest devices, are themselves the targets for an increasing variety of ASW attacks on both sides.

As for mobility on land, the American technical publications have been full of rival plans for deceiving the enemy by keeping the new and exceptionally powerful MX ICBM, of which 200 are already under construction, on the move. A 'race track' system of railway lines having been proposed, then discarded by President Carter, the latest idea is to have groups of some twenty-three shelters between which each of the missiles would be constantly shifted. Various possibilities of antiballistic missile defences (ABM) are also being revived.

THE BRITISH NUCLEAR DETERRENT

The much discussed question of the replacement of the British 'nuclear deterrent' cannot reasonably be answered without taking all these international developments of nuclear arms into account. From the point of view of the technicians and skilled personnel of the Royal Navy, who are familiar with the workings of the present system and its dependence upon United States technology, the most obvious solution, when the hulls of the existing Polaris boats become obsolete — which can hardly be much later than 1990 — would be to replace them with their most recent successors in the US Navy. Hence, despite a spate of learned discussions in strategic and academic circles (IISS, RIIA, RUSI, etc.) it is not surprising to learn that the British Cabinet is to choose the Trident missile system; a decision which was announced in the House of Commans by Mr Francis Pym in July 1980.

Arguments against this solution are: (1) the cost, and (2) the question whether the most powerful 'city-busting missiles' such as those of the American Trident system are really the most suitable contribution which Britain could make to NATO's nuclear defence of the European theatre. In fact, if a way could be found, as Lord Carver, the former Chief of the General Staff suggested, to integrate the British into that system of defence, which is to rely upon cruise missiles and intermediate-range ballistic missiles (Tomahawks and Pershing 2s), they would be of more value to the Alliance than by possessing a few maximum-size strategic missiles, which few believe would ever be launched except in retaliation, if London or other British cities had already been destroyed. I doubt whether the costing of such alternatives as the launching of cruise missiles from wide-bodied commercial jet aircraft has been fully examined. After all, the British nuclear contribution to NATO consisted for a long time of a fleet of Vulcan bombers, which served their day. The Secretary of Defence, Mr Pym, estimated in the House of Commons in July 1980 that the cost of procuring and developing five new ballistic missile nuclear submarines would be between £4000 million and £5000 million at today's prices spread over ten to fifteen years. If inflation is taken into account, the total is likely to be between £5000 million and £6850 million. The annual maintenance of the boats, to judge from the £165 million which the Polaris force costs at present, would be no great strain on a total defence budget now running at £10 785 million a year. But the huge capital expenditure on the proposed Trident replacement might, I fear, break the camel's back. It would, according to some expert opinion, mean sacrificing the sound principle that Britain should provide, as it now does, a balanced contribution to the forces of the Atlantic Alliance, in Germany, in the Atlantic, in the Channel and in the air, because of the economies which would have to be made. I believe the price to be too high. National *amour propre* and a desire not to leave France as the only strategic nuclear power in Europe, play a large part in English debate on this subject. It is a thousand pities that such primitive sentiments on this side of the Channel and French pride and insularity of outlook on the other continue to frustrate the clearly desirable and practicable co-operation of the two old European rivals and allies, who, despite passing tantrums, share so noble a naval tradition and so evident a common interest. At the very least it would make better economic sense to have replaced the Polaris boats with four or five new ones, and to continue to rely on Polaris missiles fitted with the improved and hardened warheads which are the result of the Polaris Improvement Programme, Operation *Chevaline*.

TACTICAL NUCLEAR WEAPONS (TNWs)

There remains one aspect of possible nuclear war between the Warsaw Pact and NATO for which no satisfactory strategy has yet been devised on the Western side; it is how and when to use tactical nuclear weapons. The problem is that, unless a commander in the field could be authorised to order their use when under extreme pressure from an advancing enemy, they are likely to be valueless. The British Corps, the BAOR for instance, has three regiments equipped with Lance TNWs. What to do with them if confronted with a great surge of tanks? At present a decision by the President of the United States is required before they, or any United States or other allied units in Germany could use them. If authority to use these weapons were delegated to SACEUR and by him to his subordinate commanders, they might well have, if not a decisive effect, an important delaying effect. For, though all armoured fighting vehicles of the Warsaw Pact with their crews have the best available protection against nuclear radiation, fighting for any length of time in protective clothing could be exhausting. But the inevitable nuclear response by the Soviets with the possibility of missile attacks on American cities would make a swift decision by the political figure in the White House difficult and doubtful; and I believe that General Hackett and his collaborators in their imaginative book *The Third World War* are right in concluding that, even under great stress, SACEUR would refrain from asking the President to give the fateful decision. We should face the uncomfortable fact that the decision by NATO to introduce nuclear weapons into the battlefield will be continually postponed. It would be an entirely different matter if the Warsaw Pact were the first to use nuclear weapons of any grade; I believe that SACEUR should be empowered in advance to order the use of tactical nuclear weapons, in that event, in any situation where they might be of value to the defence.

One thing is clear to me. While it is right and necessary to continue, like Sisyphus, to push the heavy weight of nuclear arms uphill in the hope of reaching the summit of disarmament, the prospect of the shameless load rolling down to earth again is so nearly certain that it would be madness for any government which is now equipped with nuclear power to relinquish it.

13 The Northern theatre of operations

It is in the extreme north of the area covered by the North Atlantic Treaty that the most concentrated core of the potential enemy's world-wide offensive power is to be found; and it confronts the weakest link in the chain of NATO defences. That is the measure of the Atlantic Allies' problem. The NATO Commands immediately affected are that of the Commander-in-Chief Allied Forces Northern Europe (Oslo) and the whole northern sea expanse of SACLANT (Norfolk, Va.), including the islands of Greenland, Iceland, Svalbard, Shetland and the Faroes. To refer to this, the main source of the Soviets' oceanic operations, simply as a 'flank' or peripheral feature of NATO's European land warfare theatre is seriously to misjudge its strategic importance.

The centre of the great military complex is the Kola Peninsula, with Murmansk less than one hundred miles from the Norwegian frontier, Pechenga, a commercial port on the Petsamo Fjord, Polyarni, the submarine base, and Severomansk, HQ of the Commander-in-Chief of the Soviet Northern Fleet, which are ice-free throughout the year. There are forty military and naval airfields on the Peninsula. The shipbuilding yards of Arkhangelsk and Severodvinsk, with its great submarine building organization, the nuclear missile testing ground of Novaya Zemblya and many other industrial and military centres and ports along the western part of the Northern Sea Route, kept open with powerful ice-breakers, are closely linked with this same complex. It is from this great *place d'armes* that the Soviet Union could launch the host of attack submarines, surface warships and long-range aircraft which could wreck the Atlantic Allies' maritime communications, unless the US aircraft carriers and the Allies' submarines, interceptor planes and ASW array could be deployed in time, and in sufficient force, to intercept them. It is from this zone also that most of the Soviets' strategic nuclear missiles (ICBMs and SLBMs) could be fired across the North Polar region to hit targets in the United States. This area of concentrated naval, military and industrial development forms part of the Soviet Union's 'Northern Theatre of Operations'; it includes Leningrad, from which the railway runs to Murmansk, and the powerful Baltic Fleet. A canal, recently widened, joins the White Sea and the Baltic, so that destroyers and other ships up to 5200 tons can be moved for service or overhaul as required, between the two fleets. Apart from the fleets with their naval aircraft, including Backfire and Badger bombers, the strategic rocket forces and border troops, the Leningrad Military District, which takes in the whole of this area, houses the 6th Army Headquarters and disposes of eight motor rifle divisions (of which two are normally in the Kola Peninsula), a tank divsion, an airborne division, a naval infantry division, and the 13th Air Army with 300 aircraft.

The Northern Fleet has 500 surface combat ships of which 60 are major units, 171 submarines, of which 91 are nuclear powered, and 90 per cent of the Soviets' SLBM force. The Baltic Fleet maintains a five to one superiority over all NATO warships in the Baltic sea. It has about 50 surface combat units, 30 conventionally-powered attack submarines, a wealth of fast attack craft, 190 fixed-wing aircraft of which 75 are missile-equipped, and many landing craft. Six of the old diesel-powered ballistic missile submarines are now attached to the fleet. Reinforcement from the neighbouring Baltic Military District could be swiftly effected. Professor Erickson summarises the situation thus:

> The result of this military, industrial and political activity has been to implement one of the strongest — possibly the strongest — complex of bases in the world in the immediate neighbourhood of northern Norway, having strategic forces capable of, and committed to, operating far beyond the Soviet periphery, plus tactical forces deployed to protect these bases and embodying the capability of seizing and holding any appreciable buffer zone in order to guarantee that self-same protection.[1]

THE OCEANIC THREAT

In considering what NATO has done and could do to deter and, if necessary, offer effective resistance to an offensive Soviet operation issuing from this Northern citadel, we must make an estimate of the character and purpose of such an offensive and what would be most likely to dissuade the Soviet Union from undertaking it. We must realise that the distinctive menace of the hitting power concentrated in the Soviet Union's Northern Theatre of Operations is that, unlike that confronting the Central German Front or the Allied forces in the Mediterranean and Near East, it is aimed directly at the United States. It is primarily an oceanic and intercontinental menace.

Consequently the immediate response to any hostile moves by the Soviet either in the extreme North or the Baltic Approaches or the neighbouring seas must be the deployment of the maximum air and sea power of the United States and its Atlantic allies, including their naval nuclear potential. This task, which fulls mainly upon the American and British navies and airforces is discussed at the end of this chapter. At present the only defensive preparation in the area envisaged by NATO appears to be the minimum which can be spared for the land and air defence of Norwegian and Danish territory, including the prepositioning of stocks for eventual reinforcement, and precautions for mining the Straits. The refusal of both governments to have either allied troops or nuclear weapons stationed in their countries in peace-time is a great impediment. Co-operation in the local defence of northern Norway, Denmark and Schleswig-Holstein is, of course, a moral and political necessity and must be as effective as possible. We shall see below what is planned for this purpose. But though the difficult and detailed co-ordination with the local armies, home guards air forces and navies of the relatively small Canadian, British and Netherlands units available is at present the main function of the Commander-in-Chief. Allied Forces Northern Europe, it is clearly not by these means that the aggressive strategy of the Soviet North can be successfully deterred or contained.

Looked at from the Soviet side it seems unlikely that the risk of war with the United States and its allies would be taken, simply for the purpose of obliging Norway and Denmark to yield the 'buffer zone' to which Erickson refers, namely the limited amount of territory in Finnmark and the Baltic Approaches required to give 'elbow room' or local security to the offensive apparatus of the Northern Theatre of Operations. It is more likely that, if there is an atmosphere of political weakness and indecision in the West, Moscow would play the 'Nordic Balance' card, with which President Urho Kekkonen of Finland is an adept practitioner, offering for instance, in exchange for the demilitarisation of northern Norway, the neutralisation of the Danish — Swedish straits and the exclusion of any German units from southern Denmark, to leave undisturbed the existing defensive alignments of Norway and Denmark with the West and Finland with the Soviet Union and the neutrality of Sweden. The old bait of declaring the Baltic a non-nuclear sea — revived as lately as 1975 — might be thrown in for good measure. While the poltroonery of politicians is not to be under-estimated, it is probable that, given sufficient evidence of American and British backing for Norwegian patriotism, which is very real, such a manoeuvre would fail.

The assumption, therefore, must be that, only if the Soviet High Command really intended a major offensive against the Western Alliance would they set out, as a preliminary, to seize the buffer zone which, once the fat was in the fire, would almost certainly involve over-running Finnish Lapland and violating Swedish neutrality, as well as seizing Denmark and key points in the vast land-mass of Norway. Given the extreme disparity in local forces, the probability of this aggression succeeding must be envisaged; but would the CPSU be prepared to face the reckoning?

If they could be made to realise that it would involve all-out war with the United States and its allies, it would be madness for them not to refrain from the fatal decision. There can, I believe, be little doubt that Article 5 of the Atlantic Treaty would very quickly be invoked and that a state of war between the Atlantic allies and the Warsaw Pact would result. If nuclear weapons were used by the Soviet forces, either at sea or on land, it can be taken as certain that the President of the United States would authorise resort to a nuclear response, at least at the tactical or intermediate level. But if, as is possible, the Soviet Union were not to take the nuclear initiative, would the President authorise the use of nuclear arms even if the tide of war were flowing against us? (The French and British would probably only do so in retaliation for an actual nuclear attack on their own territory or vessels.) In the existing state of moral antipathy to nuclear warfare it would be improbable — and the Soviets must be aware of this — unless public opinion were violently aroused against the aggressor; and if there is one circumstance which is most likely to inflame American opinion, as we know from history, it is the wholesale sinking of ships in the Atlantic. That is precisely the kind of war for which the great mechanism of destruction of the Kola peninsula is designed. With the superior force of Soviet nuclear submarines strung across the Atlantic shipping lines and many of them hovering off the eastern coast of the United States, as they would be before the outbreak of war, there would almost certainly be a series of dramatic sinkings, both of the convoys (whose probable routes were tracked and followed by the Soviet Navy in its great Okean 75 exercise) and of merchant shipping in the first week or two of hostilities. There could be no surer way of ensuring that the whole weight of American power, including in all probability nuclear power, would be thrown against the Soviet Union than for it to launch the naval and air operations of unprecedented magnitude for which its northern arsenal is equipped. This prospect, if understood by the Soviet High Command, would be the most effecitve deterrent; much more than the hurried despatch of small reinforcements to Denmark and Norway.

LOCAL DEFENCE AND REINFORCEMENT

Though I believe it to be a fallacy, however, to suppose that the strategic threat to the Atlantic allies, and the United States in particular, posed by the accumulation of naval, air and nuclear power in the Soviets' Northern Theatre of Operations can be exorcised by the readiness of the Norwegians and Danes to defend themselves and the small elements of land and air forces dedicated by SACEUR to the Northern Europe Command, it is extremely important to improve as far as possible the efficiency of the local resistance to attack. For no one can be sure that the prospect of a massive strategic response will itself deter the Soviet Union from launching their great naval offensive from the north, and that the temptation to execute the political manoeuvres and military plans, which have no doubt been prepared in detail, for dominating Scandinavia and the Baltic will not be too strong. Any violation of the territorial integrity of Denmark or Norway would be the necessary signal for collective action by bringing Article 5 of the North Atlantic Treaty into play: if therefore that local aggression could be deterred, the signal would be prevented and the chain of fatal consequences averted.

The strength of the Norwegian Army is 20 000 and of the Reserves, which it claims could be very quickly mobilised, 120 000. There is an airforce of 10 000 men, half conscripts, half volunteers, with 119 combat aircraft and 18 000 men in the Reserve. The great length of this mountainous country makes the rapid movement or concentration of land forces difficult; hence the particular importance of the Home Guard, 85 000 strong, mostly young and middle-aged men and women, all of whom have had a period of service with one of the three regular forces and keep their uniforms and weapons at home. The navy (9000 men and 22 000 reserves, including the Coastguards) has, as its chief asset, some 46 fast attack craft with Penguin SSMs or torpedoes as well as 15 submarines, a few frigates and corvettes and 30 coastal batteries. In the far north, where, it is presumed, the main Soviet offensive would come, with a sea-borne attack by at least one of the motor rifle divisions in the Kola pensinsula and land attack by another across Finland in the Kirkenes area, the Norwegians have a brigade group of three infantry battalions. Equipment for another brigade which could be flown up from the south in less than 24 hours has been pre-positioned in the North. There are 16 airfields in this area but only three of them with underground and hardened shelters for aircraft and low-level defences. There is a squadron of intercept fighters and a squadron of 15 bombers at Bodo. There is a lack of sufficient SAMs and electronic counter-measures. It is doubtful whether the airfields and early warning systems would survive more than a day or two the weight of air attack which must be anticipated.

It is obvious that the prospect of holding up an invasion depends upon the extent and speed of allied reinforcement and, unless the Norwegian Government could be persuaded to suspend its commitment against the stationing of foreign troops in the country and allow reinforcements to arrive during the period of tension, there would be little hope of their arriving in time. Pre-positioning of heavy equipment, of which a beginning has been made, would, of course, greatly reduce the delay, if sufficient aircraft were available for troop-carrying. Only on that condition does it seem likely that two of the largest contingents planned for coming to the aid of Norway could arrive in time — the Canadian Brigade, which is definitely designed for that purpose, and a brigade of the United States Marine Corps which might be made available. The former takes thirty days, the latter two weeks, to be deployed. The most immediate help would come from the United Kingdom — Netherlands Royal Marine Commando Brigade which should be able to land 7000 men in eight days. It has the great advantage that a large proportion of the force has had rigorous training in Northern Norway and is accustomed to operate on skis during the Arctic winter. The oversnow vehicles are already stockpiled on the spot. It consists of a brigade headquarters, four British Royal Marine Commandos, an amphibious group of the Royal Netherlands Marine Corps, amphibious shipping, combat helicopters and logistic support. This force comes under SACLANT and its mission includes reinforcement of Denmark and the Atlantic islands. Some of SACEUR's Allied Mobile Force consisting of three battalion groups with logistic support might also be available, but it could also be needed on the Southern Flank of NATO. It could deploy in four to seven days, and its air components (four squadrons) could be deployed in three days. Nevertheless the experience of the German invasion of Norway in 1940 and the speed with which it was accomplished, despite British and French Intervention bodes ill when faced with the possibility of a Soviet attack with greatly superior forces.

The Danish national forces, though nearly as numerous as the Norwegian (34 650 as against 39 000) are of more doubtful value. Military service is only for nine months, but on the other hand two-thirds of the officers and other ranks are not conscripts. There is also a Home Guard of 71 000 whose morale is good. The great difference, apart from the flatness of the land which makes it suitable for tank warfare as against the Norwegian mountains, is that the defence of the southern part of the country is integrated with that of the German Federal Republic. Thus the Corps defending Schleswig-Holstein, the southern part of Jutland and the island of Fusen, is composed of the German 6th Armoured Division and 13th Home Defence Group, together with the Danish Jutland Mechanised Division. Amphibious attack against the long Baltic coast, for which Polish and East German forces are known to be equipped and trained, and airborne attacks on these areas are threats with which this Corps would have to cope. But it would have good hope of reinforcement from Germany.

The other task which is of primary strategic importance to the Atlantic Alliance in this area is to attempt to mine the Straits between the Baltic and the North Sea.

The international Convention of 1958 prevents Sweden or Denmark from interfering with the innocent passage of ships in peacetime. What the Allies could do would be to mine the Danish territorial waters in each of the three international waterways in a time of crisis if (as is by no means certain) the factions in the Danish Government agreed to it. On the outbreak of war the international passages could be mined (e.g. by United States B52s) in a matter of hours. All this is the responsibility of the Baltic Approaches sub-command of the Northern Europe Command (BALTAP). It is fairly obvious that ability to move into the North Sea being of such crucial importance to the cruisers and submarines of the Soviet Baltic Fleet, a *blitzkrieg* attack to secure control of the Danish share of, at least, the Kattegat and the Sound, must be expected in the first 24 hours of hostilities. Airforce *desants* on air-fields in Southern Norway must also be foreseen.

This summary of the problems and possibilities of the Northern Europe Command at Oslo gives some idea of the cost to the Soviets of an initial onslaught on the two small NATO countries of the north. Added to the uncertainties of the strategic response which a major oceanic and inter-continental offensive issuing from the Soviet Union's Northern Theatre of Operations is likely to provoke, it is not unreasonable to hope that it will contribute somewhat to deter Moscow from taking the risk.

More important than adding to the co-operation envisaged for local defence, except for the need of greater speed in reinforcement, is an increase of the most powerful naval and air means of counteracting assault from the Kola peninsula and intercepting the thrust of Soviet bombers and submarines into the North Atlantic. Of the two weapons, it is the former, and particularly the supersonic Backfire, with its range of 3000 nautical miles and AS missiles, which is the more immediate danger to shipping on the outbreak of war.

The threat that Soviet submarines pose to allied shipping is of a longer-term nature than that posed by Soviet aviation. . . . The bombers could form part of an attack launched with less than a week's warning. . . . Soviet submarines would not likely be a major component of a surprise attack in the Atlantic. Relatively few of them deploy there, and their deployment in numbers sufficient for sea-lanes interdiction would itself be a critical signal of an impending Soviet attack.[2]

It seems that NATO and particularly the United States and British air and naval authorities are making substantial progress in strengthening the means of interception of both bombers and submarines, particularly in 'the northern air corridors which extend through the Barents Sea north of the Kola Peninsula, around North Cape, and down through the Norwegian Sea between Iceland and Britain or through the Denmark Straits between Iceland and Greenland'.[4] That is the strategic G-I-UK gap, where the allies' early warning and ASW systems would be put to the test. No aspect of the Atlantic allies' maritime defences is more important than these. Indeed, the most valuable contribution Norway makes to the allied cause is the NATO surveillance Station situated at North Cape which monitors all Soviet surface and sub-surface naval traffic leaving Murmansk and other Russian harbours for the open sea. This radar station would be a prime target.

14 The Central Front

It is the eyeball to eyeball confrontation of the armies and air forces of the Atlantic allies and the Warsaw Pact along the eastern border of the German Federal Republic that the word 'NATO' brings to mind in common parlance. Certainly it is this dividing line which recalls most clearly the original purpose of the North Atlantic Treaty, which was to stop the encroachment of the Red Army beyond the zone in Germany, which the Soviet Union occupied in virtue of the Yalta and Potsdam Agreements, and Czechoslovakia which, by a combination of political conspiracy and military pressure, had also been absorbed into the Communist orbit in 1948. We are studying in this book the trial of strength between the Western allies and the CPSU with its world-wide ambitions, including the strategic problems on the northern and southern flanks of this Central German front, on the seas and on other continents. But it is in this Central European theatre of operations that we find the greatest concentration of armaments and military manpower of both sides and it is here that the allies have cause to fear a mass attack by conventional forces far more numerous than their own.

It is the shortest of the three European fronts, a matter of 900 km as the crow flies from the Baltic Sea in the north to the frontiers of Austria and Switzerland. For NATO's purposes about 100 km of this line north of the Elbe, including Hamburg and Schleswig-Holstein is the responsibility of the Baltic Approaches Sub-Command of the Northern Allied Forces Command at Oslo.

The remainder, that is the bulk of the German Federal Republic, is defended by the German Bundeswehr (335 200 strong) and Air Force (106 000) and by contingents of five of its allies, the United States, the United Kingdom, Belgium, the Netherlands and Canada. The Territorial Defence Forces in Germany, with a wartime strength of 330 000 men have the task of giving logistic support to all the NATO fighting forces in the country as required: it would take several days only for them to leave their civilian jobs and join up. All these forces come under the Commander-in-Chief Allied Forces Central Europe, now the German Lieutenant-General Franz-Joseph Schulze.

The French, in virtue of a bilateral treaty with the German Federal Government, have two divisions and a sizeable air force stationed in south-west Germany on both sides of the Rhine; they form part of the 1st French Army with its headquarters at Strasbourg and are not integrated in the structure of NATO's Centre Europe Command. This is a great disadvantage for planning purposes, both to the French military authorities and to NATO. French liaison staffs are attached to the principal NATO headquarters and there are regular staff conferences about the possible co-operation of French land and air forces in this region. What is needed is not the reintegration of French forces under the command of SACEUR, which is politically impossible, but a clear reassurance by the French President that an attack upon Germany would automatically bring France to its aid under Article 5 of the Atlantic Treaty, as indeed President de Gaulle himself promised it would. This would assure the French officers concerned that the detailed contingency plans which they are making with their Allied colleagues would have the necessary political endorsement to be activated on 'the day'. There were signs from a statement on defence put out by President Giscard d'Estaing's party in May 1980 that such approach to reality was being made. It remains to be seen how far the blinkered devotion of the Gaullistes and the Left to the dogma of national in-dependence can be overcome in the run up to the next Presidential election.

STRUCTURE OF THE CENTRE EUROPE COMMAND

The whole territory of the Federal Republic is designated as a Forward Combat Zone (FCZ) beginning at the frontier, where, for compelling reasons of policy, there must be the maximum possible resistance to an invading force, and, west of it, the Rear Combat Zone (RCZ). In the former, brigade and divisional formations, armoured cavalry regiments, etc., are deployed, with the corps areas to the west of them. In the latter are most of the supply installations of the allies concerned, Belgium and the Netherlands, with their ports, railways, roads and storage facilities, form the Communications Zone. Antwerp, for example, is the main port for the supply and reinforcement of the British Corps. For operational purposes the German Federal Republic is divided into two sectors, the Northern Army Group (NORTHAG) with its headquarters at München-Gladbach and a British Commander-in-Chief, and the Central Army Group (CENTAG) with its headquarters at Heidelberg and an American Commander-in-Chief.

The Bundeswehr, the largest of the Allied forces is, as we shall see, in position throughout the country from north to south, including the 6th Armoured Division in Schleswig-Holstein. The deployment of the American, British and French forces reflects their original zones of occupation at the end of the second World War. Thus the French are still in the Saar, Baden Baden and the upper reaches of the Rhine: the Americans in Southern Germany, Frankfurt, Mainz, Nuremberg and Northern Bavaria; the British, still called at home 'The Army of the Rhine', in the Ruhr and Lower Saxony.

Strategic needs would have dictated a different deployment. The main danger of a massive attack by the armour of the Warsaw Pact is evidently in the North German Plain, though the urban spread of the last decade has, as in other areas on the western side of the frontier, created many obstacles to the tank. It is on both sides of the Helmstadt—Dortmund Autobahn that the sharpest thrust is anticipated. In this sector, a large German Corps and the British Corps, supported by Belgian and Dutch division of uncertain fighting value would have to bear the brunt of the attack. The British Corps is numerically smaller and less favoured in the scale of reinforcements available than the United States forces, most of which are stationed in the south, an area which, because of the mountainous terrain and forests of much of its borders with the east, is less vulnerable to large-scale armoured thrusts. The French are stationed much too far from the frontier. If, as is reasonable to expect, the French divisions came to the aid of Germany in case of war, it is CENTAG which would benefit from their support. The decision last year to station an American brigade with the Northern Army Group was a step toward redressing the balance.

The present strength of the two Army Groups is as follows:

NORTHAG

1   German Corps with 4 divisions comprising 11 brigades, one -airborne brigade and a tank regiment.

1   UK Corps (BAOR) with 4 divisions, comprising 8 armoured-battalions, and an artillery division, etc.

1   Netherlands Corps (stationed in its own country) with 2 divisions, comprising 6 brigades.

1   Belgian Corps with 2 divisions, comprising 4 brigades

1   US Brigade.

CENTAG

2   German Corps (II and III) with 6 divisions comprising 16 brigades, two air-borne brigades and a tank regiment.

2   US Corps (V and VII) with 4 divisions comprising 12 brigades and armoured cavalry regiments.

1   Canadian Brigade group.

1   dual-based US mechanised division, of which 2 brigades are in Kansas, USA and a third in Germany.

1   dual-based armoured cavalry regiment.

There are two Tactical Air Forces, the 2nd and the 4th, the 2nd operating in the NORTHAG, the 4th in the CENTAG area. Their links with the commands of the land forces have hitherto been rather loose. The 2nd Tactical Air Force, which includes British, German, Belgian and Dutch squadrons, has from the start had its headquarters alongside NORTHAG, but it is only in the last year that the 4th, which includes units from the United States, Germany and Canada, has had its headquarters linked to CENTAG at Heidelberg. More important, the over-all air command, AAFCE, now has joint headquarters with those of the Commander-in-Chief Central Europe, which is continually manned on a 24-hour basis. The number of aircraft available to the Atlantic allies in Central and Northern Europe, without reinforcement, is 2350, or 2790 if the French squadrons are included, as against 4200 of the Warsaw Pact.[1]

LONG-TERM DEFENCE

It is in this Central Region that the full weight of the Warsaw Pact's superiority in conventional arms is most apparent. The great question is whether the quality of the Atlantic Allies in capacity and skill, including the latest devices of electronic warfare can make up for the disparity in the number of armoured fighting vehicles, artillery, airborne forces, tactical aircraft and missiles; and whether — as some authorities believe[2] — the latest precision-guided anti-tank missiles and surface-to-air missiles give a decisive advantage to the defence.

Nothing has happened, however, to modify Admiral Lord Hill-Norton's conclusion two years ago (see p. 79) that the Warsaw Pact's superiority in conventional strength has nearly reached the dangerous ratio of three to one. We have taken stock (in chapter 7) of the standing strength of the Soviet Union's Groups of Forces in the German Democratic Republic, in Czechoslovakia and in Poland and of the neighbouring Military Districts of the Soviet Union. President Brezhnev's withdrawal of 1000 tanks and 20 000 men announced in his Berlin speech of 6 October 1979, adroit political move as it was, has made only a marginal difference to the balance of strength.

On the other hand a good deal has been done by the major Atlantic Allies in the last three years to modernise their armoury and increase the effectiveness of their conventional forces, as well as committing themselves to the new theatre nuclear force in order to counteract the Soviet Union's ominous preponderance. The decision taken by the North Atlantic Council in July 1977 to require an increase of three per cent in real money in each of its members' defence budgets has at least put an end to the petty reductions of the forces, and the Long-Term Defence Programme adopted in 1978 has produced some continous progress. Ten 'task forces' have since been at work to plan the greater readiness of the Alliance. It is a development which marks a turning point in the history of NATO and, while they concern every theatre of operations on land, in the air or at sea, I will record here their terms of reference, all of which (except No 4) have a direct bearing on the defensive needs of this Centre Europe Command.

1. Short-term readiness, including rapid out-loading of ammunition and chemical protection.
2. Rapid reinforcement by United States, United Kingdom and Canadian Strategic Reserves, including the use of civil air and sea lifts and the addition of three sets of divisional

equipment for United States reinforcements (POMCUS) in Europe.

3. Increased reserves and improved mobilisation techniques.
4. Co-operative measures (including, especially, command, control and communications) at sea and national naval force increases particularly in ASW, mine-warfare and defence against air and surface attack.
5. Air defence integration and qualitative improvement.
6. Communications, Command and Control (C3).
7. Electronic warfare improvement on land, at sea and in the air.
8. Consumer logistics, including an improvement in war reserve stocks and greater alliance co-ordination of logistic support.
9. Rationalisation of the research, development and production of armaments in the direction of standardisation and interoperability.
10. Theatre nuclear modernisation.

FORWARD DEFENCE

General Schulze in a recent summary of the task imposed by geography on his Command[3] shows the necessity of 'forward defence' and his confidence in the power of its modernised air forces to make a reality of it.

The Central Region ... concomitantly suffers from a lack of depth in its defence. This is one, but only one of the reasons why we have focussed our planning on a refinement of the concept of forward defence. We simply cannot afford to pursue a defensive strategy excessively flexible, in the sense of trading ground — and population — in order to gain time, or to preserve our forces and rely on a massive counter-attack. Forward defence, on the other hand, does not mean static defence, quite the contrary. The success of our forward defence will depend on our ability to bring all available fire power to bear, from the very outset of hostilities in a well co-ordinated, truly 'combined land — air battle'. The immense fire power, the great flexibility and the long reach of our air forces give them a special part to play in breaking up the momentum of the enemy's attack and isolating his attacking spear-heads from their follow-on formations.

He goes on to describe recent increases in anti-tank and air-defence power, urgently required 'in view of the some 20 000 tanks arrayed against the Region and the great increase in offensive capability of the Warsaw Pact air forces'.

> Our new medium and long-range anti-tank missile systems, including anti-tank helicopters, augmented by the considerable combat power of the A-10 aircraft, present a formidable array, and this will continue to improve. The extensive dialogue in Soviet military journals enables us to appreciate the problem facing a potential aggressor as a result of the growing effectiveness of our anti-tank defence, which could frustrate the classic break-through in which the Soviets so firmly believe.

General Schulze then summarises the allies' progress in air defence, the advent of the F-15 air-superiority fighters, the new short-range air-defence weapons, Roland, Rapier and Gepard and SAM missiles:

> The NIKE high altitude and HAWK medium altitude systems are deployed in two overlapping belts. This belt concept is another new feature of the Central Region. It provides not only for a surface-to-air missile coverage from almost ground level up to 100,000 feet, but it ensures the integration of our national resources. This system is supported by an integrated Air Defence Ground Environment comprising strike and mobile early-warning and air defence radar, Controlled Reporting Centres and Sector Operating Centres. It is internationally manned and provides minute-to-minute command and control over the interceptor fighters and surface-to-air missile systems. The airborne early warning system AWACS will compensate for the vulnerability of the ground-based system.

ARMS AND THE MAN

I have quoted these extracts of the Commander-in-Chief's summary of some recent developments in the Central Region because it is right to be reminded of the pugnacity and confidence of the military and the progress made in providing them with new weapons to counteract the massive superiority in numbers of the Warsaw Pact. There are, of course, many other types of armament required by the Atlantic allies' forces in this unequal contest, beginning with the modernisation and increase of their tanks, for the tank itself remains the best anti-tank weapon. But, unlike the mass production of the Soviet Union's arms factories, new tanks take the Western allies years to produce. It is a task upon which all the major allies defence ministries are engaged and in which the perennial fight for standardisation or interoperability against the ingrained habits and interests of national arms manufacturers continues. Thus the British ministry finds arguments for preferring a new heavy main battle tank (80) and a better, rifled gun of its own to sharing, as the French are doing, in the production of the faster German Leopard II, which will come into general service with the *Bundeswehr* at least five years before the British Army can hope to see its new heavy-weight. The Americans have also produced a very effective tank of their own, the XMI, but have agreed with the Germans and the French to adopt the same 120 mm smooth bore gun, so that the same ammunition can be used. This is just one typical example of the national and professional rivalries which surround the planning of any major weapon of land, sea or air warfare. Often, however, the ever-rising cost of production compels international co-operation as it did in the case of the Tornado; because of inflation, this is likely to become more and more the rule.

The first requirement of a defensive alliance of free peoples is a fighting spirit, however. Certainly I would say, from my own experience, that General Schulze's dedication is reflected in that of the German, British and American troops under his command and the small Canadian contingent. The same is true of the French Staff Officers, whom I have met both in Germany and in France. The Belgian and Dutch Corps have inevitably felt the influence of the recurrent moves at home to reduce military service. In the case of the Dutch, the fact that they are all normally stationed in their own country — apart from the difficulty of moving them up in time of crisis to their unfamiliar forward positions on the Elbe — makes them particularly exposed to an unfavourable political atmosphere.

THE BRITISH ARMY OF THE RHINE

The morale and fighting qualities of the British Corps are of immediate interest to us. It has benefited greatly from the restructuring which began in 1976; and the increase in pay and allowances, brought about by the Thatcher government in 1979, have eased the economic conditions of this wholly volunteer force and its families. There are in all 158 000 British service personnel and dependents in Germany, of whom 40 000 are children. The peacetime strength of the British Corps which could be quickly trebled by the addition of reserve units, if war threatened, is 48 275, of whom, at any one time, about 4000 officers and men are helping to fight terrorism in Northern Ireland. This is no negligible inconvenience; for though they could, in principle, be brought back in one or two days, it is certain that an intensification of the IRA's subversive violence in Ulster would be stimulated by the Soviet Union as part of its preparation for a military offensive. The Royal Air Force have eleven squadrons in the 2nd Allied Tactical Air Force, which has a British Commander, including two squadrons of Harriers for close support of the British Corps. It also provides Wessex helicopters for the army.

There are, in addition, 2820 British soldiers and airmen in the Berlin garrison, under the 'Four Power Status' of the city. They form no part of the NATO Command in Germany, but they (with their American and French colleagues) are covered by the North Atlantic Treaty, so that any attack on them would bring Article 5 of the treaty into play. Planted in the centre of the most important of the satellite countries of the Soviet Union, they have freedom of communication and, given all the electronic devices now available, they inevitably constitute an advanced observation post of the utmost value. It would evidently be necessary for the Soviet High Command to endeavour to take out this nuisance at the start of hostilities.

The Corps, as now organised,[4] consists of four armoured divisions and one field force, supported by an artillery division, the Corps Engineers with their amphibious regiment and bridging equipment; three signals regiments and an aviation squadron to provide communications. Each of the four armoured divisions has two armoured regiments (battalions) equipped with some sixty-four *Chieftains*, which since 1966 have been the standard British Battle tanks. The Chieftain has latterly had an improved fire-control system and there are plans to replace it during the 1980s with some of the new Chieftains ordered by the hapless Shah (Challengers) fitted with Chobham armour and, at the end of the decade[5] with the new heavy MBT which I have mentioned. Supplementing each tank battalion is an armoured reconnaissance regiment equipped with Scorpions and Scimitars, which are light tanks with 76 mm guns. Four mechanised infantry companies in each division are carried in armoured personnel carriers of some antiquity (F.V.432): but a brand-new APC is promised 'in the 1980s'. Wombat anti-tank weapons are mounted on the APCs and each infantry platoon is to receive one of the more effective Milan guided missiles. The artillery divisions have a variety of guns, of 175 mm, 105 mm and 155 mm calibre, and anti-tank missiles, four batteries of Lance nuclear missiles and two air defence groups equipped with Rapier missiles and soon to have Blindfire radar.

It is the same story throughout the armoury of the British Corps — gradual replacement of familiar weapons with new ones which take considerable periods to produce. Thus in the artillery group, to quote Mr N.L. Dodd, 'The new FH70 Anglo-German-Italian 155 mm. towed gun is coming into service to replace the older 155 mm. guns.' 'It is hoped that in the late 1980s the Abbot 105 will be replaced by the SP model of the FH70 now under development.' 'The combat engineer regiments are presently receiving the highly effective and versatile Combat Engineer Tractor.' 'The new Medium Girder Bridge is now entering service.' 'Aviation squadrons have received the Gazelle AH's in place of the older Sioux.' 'Command and control on the battlefield will be much improved by the Wavell automatic data processing aid to staff work. . . . It is expected to enter service in the early 1980s.' And so on. These few examples give some idea of the complexity of the modern army and its impedimenta (alas for the days of muskets and horses!), of the strain which the constant changes — and promised changes — of equipment impose upon the officers, NCOs, gunners, drivers, mechanics, signal personnel, electrical and mechanical engineers and infantrymen and the high level of technical expertise required in the day-to-day work of the British Corps. It is, I imagine, a marked contrast to the competence needed to handle the mass-produced and standardised weapons and equipment of the Soviet Army.

There are other aspects of the British Army's life in Germany which deserve special attention. One, which applies *mutatis mutandis* to the Americans, is the cost and practical difficulties of accommodating and training a large body of foreign soldiers and their families and educating their children in a country which has increasing population and housing problems of its own. For instance, the British Army and Air Force have to provide eighty-four primary schools, seven middle schools and nine secondary schools (two of them boarding schools). What is to happen to this 'camp-following' population if there is a warning of imminent attack, with convoys of troops of seven nations moving hurriedly across the country from south to north and west to east from their peace-time quarters to their forward positions, let alone re-inforcements filling every available ship and moving up by air, rail and road? This phenomenon, which has no counterpart on the Warsaw Pact side of the line, receives too little attention. Another problem of a foreign army surrounded by another people's busy civilian life is space for training. Much of the area in which the BAOR is stationed is thickly populated and manoeuvres on any considerable scale are unpopular with the locals and expensive. Nor is it only the training of the regulars which is important; 20 000 British reservists come to Germany every year for their training periods. One valuable safety-valve is the Suffield training area of 2500 square miles in Canada. Here weapons and equipment for a complete battle group are stocked, and six or seven battle groups are flown over each year for a month of extensive training. Other formations have been trained in the United States, and there are regular training visits to the British Sovereign Base areas in Cyprus. All things considered, the British Corps ranks high among the fighting forces of the Atlantic allies in Europe.

ATTACK AND WARNING

To return to the general situation of NATO in this Central German Theatre of Operations, it is necessary to face two important issues which are closely related. One is the threat of sudden attack; another is the MBFR, the dragging discussion of mutual force reductions in Vienna.

The original notion of the Mutual Force Reduction Conversations, which eventually started in Geneva in October 1973, was that the mere confrontation of large bodies of troops along the demarcation line between West and East Germany and Czecho- slovakia was itself a cause of dangerous tension which must be relaxed. This is, in fact, a very questionable proposition; a much more real danger of hostilities comes from the rapid development of superior offensive striking power in land and air arms, both conventional and nuclear. The negotiating team on the NATO side in the MBFR has been the United States, Federal Germany, Britain, Belgium, Holland and Luxemburg, with France eschewing the palaver and other European allies having observer status. The team on the Warsaw Pact side consists of the Soviet Union, the German Democratic Republic and Czechoslovakia. The NATO team have stuck throughout six years of inconclusive negotiation to the simple issue of manpower, largely because, amid the complexity of weapon systems, it seemed the only basis on which numerical parity could be obtained. But it was mainly to satisfy pacific elements in Western public opinion and most of all to meet the demand of the US Congress for a reduction in the number of the 300 000 Americans serving in Europe — a demand which has since disappeared.

The idea was to trade progressive reductions in US manpower for equivalent reductions of Russians on the other side. But no agreement could be reached upon the actual number of Warsaw Pact troops. It has suited the delaying tactics of the Soviet bloc to pretend that a condition of parity already exists between the forces of East and West in what is called the 'guidelines area'. Their negotiators in June 1976 gave the total of their ground forces as 805 000 as against the official NATO estimate of 962 000 and they stick to that position. On that basis they proposed equal reductions on either side, which in fact would only increase their relative superiority over the Atlantic Alliance forces.

But this is only shadow boxing. If the negotiations are kept in being it is because both sides see in them a certain political propaganda value according to their very different objectives of *détente*. A doubtfully prudent offer by NATO in 1975 to widen the area of negotiation by including in its contribution 1000 nuclear warheads (from what was believed at the time to be its superiority in the number of TNWs) lay dormant until it was revived by the North Atlantic Council in December 1979 as part of a proposed package deal for a mutual limitation of theatre nuclear forces. There is no sign at present that anything will come of it. Senator Sam Nunn, however, an able strategist, who has long been the advocate of forward defence on the Central Front, believes that some use could be made of MBFR to reduce the threat of sudden attack. He said at a recent German — American conference:[6]

> The consequences of a Warsaw Pack invasion attended by little or no warning are profound for NATO. It is to the Alliance's credit that its Long Term Defence Programme, if fully implemented, will enhance NATO's capacity to resist a surprise attack. Yet, if the resolution of the problem posed by reduced warning is to be the central objective of NATO force planning, a restoration of adequate warning time must be the Alliance's paramount arms control aim in Vienna. The preservation of the existing conventional balance in Europe at lower force levels would provide no guarantee against the threat of an attack without warning. ... The time is long overdue to shift our primary focus at MBFR from reducing the presence of military forces in Central Europe to one of precluding their being employed in a sudden and unexpected manner. This means focussing on the creation of a control regime that would make surprise attack impossible.

I am not very sanguine about inducing the Soviet Command of the Warsaw Pact forces to submit to a system of 'permanent and pervasive on site inspection in Europe', such as Senator Nunn proposed, and I am a little doubtful of its popularity with the Military Committee of NATO or the French General Staff. There is of course a possibility of the 'Confidence Building' measures included in the resolutions of the Helsinki Conference on Security and Co-operation in Europe (notificiation of manoeuvres; invitation of observers etc.) being operated less stingily by the Soviet military authorities. It all depends upon how sweetly, at any given time, it suits the CPSU to sing the siren song of Peaceful Coexistence. I should doubt if this could have more value on the Western side than that of gaining a little time. For my part I put greater faith in the maximum use of the Allies' intelligence services in order to acquire advance information and in making sure that their findings really reach the effective policy-makers in each government.[7] For the history of the initial surprise attacks in the wars of the twentieth century shows that their success has almost always been due more to the unpreparedness of politicans than to the faults of the military.

15 The Southern theatre of operations

The Southern theatre of possible conflict between the Soviet Union and the Atlantic Alliance covers the whole of the south of the European continent and Asia Minor as well as the Mediterranean, Adriatic, Aegean and Black Seas, an area roughly 4000 km long from east to west. We shall see later the sections of the Soviet forces in the neighbouring Military Districts of the Soviet Union and the southern tier of the Warsaw Pact which would be involved, with the navy, in any military offensive in this area. On the NATO side, the responsibility for defending the Allied territories and simultaneously fighting the enemy within this great area — for action by the Soviet squadron in the Mediterranean would inevitably synchronise from the start with land and air attacks from the north — rests primarily upon the Commander-in-Chief Allied Forces Southern Europe with his headquarters in Naples, at present Admiral Harold E. Shear, US Navy.

It is a more varied and complex task than that confronting NATO on the Central German Front or in the Northern Theatre of Operations. Politically, the lack of cohesion between the Allied nations concerned — France, Italy, Greece, Turkey and the United States — is even more marked. Britain is virtually an absentee. Spain, though a likely candidate for membership of the Atlantic Alliance, is at present impeded from active co-operation by internal opposition. Of the twelve other Mediterranean states, two — Egypt and Israel — are at present well-disposed to the West; four others could be regarded as benevolently neutral; six as malevolent, and in two cases at least, Libya and Syria, potential bases for the Soviet air forces. The conflict between the United States, with their commitment to the support of Israel, and the European Community, whose reliance on Arab oil disposes them to espouse the rights of the Palestinians, has added a new com-

160

plexion to the perennial problems of the Middle East. All the eighteen Mediterranean states, of course, are dependent to some extent on the sea for their economic life. On any day over 1500 ocean-going ships and about 5000 smaller vessels are moving across these waters, including an increasing number of Soviet merchantmen; and, though the super-tankers from the Gulf circumnavigate the African Continent, a great deal of the oil which is essential to western Europe and the United States still comes through the Suez Canal and from North Africa. These are some of the political and economic background facts which condition and complicate defensive planning. It is a task of diffuse defence with effective co-ordination as its distinctive problem.

There is, however, one massive fact which may itself be a decisive deterrent to an offensive by the CPSU in this theatre. It is the United States 6th Fleet, which Admiral Shear its Commander-in-Chief is justified as describing as 'the most modern powerful naval fighting force in the world today, the genuine cutting edge of our military capability in this region and a force absolutely indispensable in our ability to protect the southern front.'[1] Without the 6th Fleet, the Soviet High Command might very well be tempted to seize the opportunity, which the political disarray of its adversaries' offers in the eastern Mediterranean, to implement the strategy of a 'deep envelopment of NATO'. For the hitting power of the 6th Fleet is not only naval: the most vital industrial centres of the Soviet Union are well within the range of its nuclear missiles, and nuclear-armed carrier-borne aircraft.

BALANCE OF FORCES

Apart from this major asset and whatever contribution France might make to the common defence, NATO, if it came to war, would, on the face of it, have an advantage in manpower, 560 000 as opposed to 400 000 of the Warsaw Pact. On the other hand the Pact would have a numerical superiority in the air, with a front-line air strength of 1500 plus the 300 aircraft of the Black Sea Fleet's naval air force and Backfire bombers from their bases in the Crimea. As against this NATO would have 950 planes supplemented by those of the 6th Fleet Aircraft Carriers; though the Central Front necessarily has the first claim on reinforcement of the Atlantic Alliance tactical air power it is clearly urgent to add strength in the next few years to the two tactical air forces of the Southern Command. At sea the Soviet Union would probably have at least fifty ships in its 5th Escadra in the Mediterranean (forty-seven today) including the aircraft carrier, *Minsk*, and possibly another, missile cruisers and submarines. The total might well be doubled by reinforcement from the Northern Fleet.

For the European Atlantic Allies, the French Fleet is the most considerable and would be the main naval force in the western Mediterranean, while the land and air forces of France would presumably be absorbed in time of war in defence of the north-east of the country and southern Germany. The French Navy is outside the NATO framework, but the existing liaison system would assure co-operation with the ships of Naples Command in time of war, though an effective mechanism of communication and control would have to be quickly brought into being. It was a contribution to the needs of the Alliance that the two Clémenceau class aircraft carriers and the main part of the fleet of forty-eight surface combat vessels and twenty-seven submarines were moved from Brest to Toulon after the Martinique Conference between Presidents Ford and Giscard d'Estaing in 1975. Most of the French ships carry Exocet SSMs.

The Italian Navy, modernised at great expense in the last few years, is the most efficient of the NATO fleets. It includes three cruisers and four destroyers carrying ASW helicopters and SAM missiles, nine submarines and some twenty frigates and corvettes, a hydrofoil and four fast attack craft armed with SSMs. The most useful contribution of the Turkish and Greek Navies to the Allied strength is that of their fast attack craft with missiles.

This summary of the opposing forces in the Southern Theatre of Operations is only of very limited significance without comparison of the quality of equipment on either side. Six years ago Admiral Means Johnston Jun., then Commander-in-Chief, southern Europe, said:

I know our troops to be well-trained, well-led and highly motivated. Regrettably, however, they cannot match the other side in equipment. We are different in the quantities of supplies on hand — in many cases far below NATO levels — and we are plagued by growing obsolescence and incompatibility. Still more worrisome is the realisation that the Soviet divisions which face the Southern Region are all motorised or mechanised, whereas only six of our divisions possess such armour and mobility.[2]

Serious efforts have been made since then the improve the capability of the Turkish Army, which is the main body of the Southern Command's land forces, for armoured warfare. But the bad blood between Greece and Turkey since 1974 and the US Senate's four years' embargo upon urgently needed arms for Turkey greatly retarded in this region the progress of the armament programme agreed by the North Atlantic Council in July 1977. The state of the Italian sea, land and air forces is more satisfactory.

THE POLITICAL BACKGROUND

The political situation of the Allied forces in Southern Europe is more unfavourable than it was in the early 1970s. One serious development has been the waning influence and popularity of the United States, and this at a time when the prospect of containing a Soviet offensive against the Southern Region is more than ever dependent upon US sea power and, eventually, nuclear power.

The Iranian repudiation of what had become virtually a military alliance with the United States and the impotence of the United States and their allies to put a swift end to the outrageous detention of their diplomats as hostages were blows to the prestige of the United States. The strategic and economic consequences of the Iranian Revolution are indeed serious for the Western Alliance as a whole though the resurgence of Islamic fervour which it triggered off is, on balance, more disadvantageous to the Soviet Union than to the Atlantic Alliance. In the Mediterranean area itself there has been a chill in the political atmosphere. When the Southern Command of NATO was established in 1951 under Admiral Robert B. Carney, there was hardly a port at which a US naval ship would not be sure of a friendly reception. Now it is not only in the Aegean, where the backwash of the Greco-Turkish quarrel deprived the 6th Fleet of the use of the Piraeus and other Greek harbours, that naval facilities were denied. Malta, with its Grand Harbour, once the Naval headquarters of the Southern Command of NATO, has passed into the hands of the maverick Dom Mintoff who is sparring with the bitterly hostile Ghadafi of Libya; and Tripoli, like the other North African ports except Alexandria, is closed to any US naval visit. It is the same, but for Tel-Aviv, on the Eastern shore of the Mediterranean, where the Syrian ports are at the disposal of the Soviet squadron, and conflicting Lebanese factions can no longer be quelled by the sight of the 6th Fleet on the horizon. More seriously the French harbours are no longer open to the American Navy.

Within otherwise friendly countries variants of Left-wing or nationalist forms of anti-Americanism are at work. In Spain, with which a military defence agreement is periodically reviewed at a price, the US navy still has a base at Rota and air force facilities; but, if the Socialist Workers' Party came to power, its policy would be one of non-alignment. There is fortunately very little anti-Americanism in Italy, where the powerful Communist Party, for some reason, is not hostile to the country's membership of NATO. In Turkey the anger caused by the arms embargo has died down, and the military government has put an end to anti-American demonstrations and Communist agitation. Ismir is a secure base, other Anatolian ports are open to naval visits and, on occasion, United States ships pass through the Turkish Straits into the Black Sea. It is refreshing, for instance, to read of the courtesy visit of the guided missile cruiser *Richard K. Turner* and the destroyer *USS Lawrence* to the Romanian port of Constanta in June 1979 and of the popular welcome which they received.

The most serious political impediment to effective co-ordination of defence against Soviet aggression in this region is of course the quarrel between Greece and Turkey. It is a quarrel whose roots go far deeper than a contention between governments, for they are part of the ancestral antipathies of the peoples derived from memories of the Ottoman conquests, the Greek War of Independence and the crushing victories of Kemal Ataturk, nurtured on both sides since the 1920s by the stimulus of nationalist education and propaganda. It is this that made the consequences of the latest stage of the feud so long impervious to mediation. It is the occupation of nearly half of Cyprus by the Turkish Army since 1974 which sticks in the gullet of every Greek; and the fact that this was provoked by a clumsy Greek military attempt, in the days of the unloved 'Colonels', to secure the government of the island is forgotten. At present there seems no prospect of getting the Turkish troops out and leaving the Greek and Turkish communities to evolve a *modus vivendi*. The Cyprus crisis opened up an even more intractable dispute between Greece and Turkey over the sovereignty and exploitation of the Aegean sea-bed, strewn as it is with Greek islands up to a stone's throw off the Turkish coast and, what is even more frustration to NATO, the control of the air-space over them. The compromise which resulted in the return of Greece to NATO and the re-organization of the Allied air-command in November 1980 was a victory for good sense which owed much to the patient diplomacy of two Supreme Allied Commanders, Generals Haig and Rogers.

Turkish — American reconciliation was more rapid once the arms embargo had been lifted by Congress in September 1978. In the next month four main US bases and twenty-three other facilities in Anatolia were reactivated for surveillance and early-warning purposes.

American arms and equipment are being used to modernise the Turkish forces of 485 000 men, the second largest, after the Germans, in NATO which are short of the armoured fighting vehicles, anti-tank guns, helicopters and missiles which would be needed to repel a threat by the enemy across the bare, rolling country of Eastern Anatolia, which is suitable for tank warfare, as indeed is Eastern Thrace. It is the German Federal Republic which has come to the aid of Turkey in a big way, because of the strategic importance of strengthening this weak link in the alliance's defences. They are helping, not only with the supply of weapons — Leopard tanks, for example — and the gift of surplus material from the Bundeswehr, but also by taking the lead in a far-reaching programme of economic recovery. For Turkey was nearly bankrupt, largely because of the high cost of importing crude oil and other energy resources. The OECD has prepared this programme on the proposal of the United States, British, French and German governments. The internal situation of Turkey, however, was disturbed with fractious political parties and even more acts of terrorism by both Left and Right than bedevil Italy, Spain and other Western countries, until order was restored by the military leaders of the country.

The internal situation in Greece is not so turbulent. Its association with the EEC is working well and, though the militant socialism of Mr Papandreou and his Pasok party continues to foment an undercurrent of violent hostility to NATO and the

United States, the government of Mr Rallis, who succeeded the veteran Mr Karamanlis upon his election to the Presidency in May 1980, is convinced of the value of Greece's identification with the Western Alliance. This does not prevent the good relations which the Greek, like the Turkish Government, are at some pains to maintain with their Communist Balkan neighbours. Relations with Yugoslavia are particularly friendly and there is no sign of this being changed since the death of Tito.

ALLIED CO-OPERATION

The United States is the principal contributor to the defence of the Southern Region, in addition to the two formidable Battle Groups of the 6th Fleet centred on their great aircraft carriers. The 5th Tactical Air Force, with its headquarters at Vicenza, and the 6th with its headquarters at Ismir, both come under the orders of a US Lieutenant-General at Naples. Italian and US tactical squadrons compose the former. As to the latter, the defection of the Greeks destroyed for a time the co-operation of the three allies. leaving to the US and Turkish squadrons the defence of Turkey. Since the Greek re-integration the 6th Tactical Air Force has been divided, with the Turkish HQ remaining at Ismir and a new HQ at Larissa, in Greek Thrace with a Greek commander, both of course being under the American Commander of Allied Air Forces Southern Europe. The combined strength of the 5th and 6th Tactical Air Forces is about fifty squadrons of attack, strike and air-defence aircraft with Nike missile squadrons and Hawk missile batteries.

The Commander of Allied Naval Forces Southern Europe — other than the US 6th Fleet — which is called 'Striking and Support Forces Southern Europe' and would in wartime be committed to NATO — is an Italian Admiral. He (like SACLANT in the Atlantic), has no ships permanently assigned to his command, but twice a year he directs exercises of a multi-national task force composed of Italian, (Greek), Turkish and US ships in which a British frigate usually takes part. The main regular purpose of the Command is the surveillance of all Soviet naval vessels in the Mediterranean, through co-ordinated missions of individual ships and aircraft of the allies. The Commander of Land Forces, Southern Europe, is an Italian

General with his headquarters at Verona. The British occupy two relics of the past at each end of the Mediterranean Sea which, though not technically part of NATO, would be of value to the Alliance in time of war, Gibraltar with its dockyard, airfield and radar and the two Sovereign Base areas in Cyprus. Units of the BAOR come for training there and the RAF operates and defends the large airfield of Akrotiri. It is the maintenance of the radar and communications facilities, originally created for help to CENTO, which is probably the most useful British contribution to the Allied cause in this area. A recent development is the provision of a mobile force under SACEUR which can be despatched at short notice to support the defence of either flank, north or south of NATO in Europe, like the United Kingdom — Netherlands Royal Marine Commando of SACLANT, whose value for reinforcement in Northern Norway we mentioned in chapter 13. From time to time the mobile force joins forces of the Southern Command for an exercise, like the large amphibious attack on Sardinia practised in May 1980, witnessed by the author.

SOVIET DEPLOYMENT AND PROBABLE OBJECTIVES

Such, in outline is the mechanism of defence of the Atlantic Alliance in its far-flung Southern Region. We must now consider the objectives of the Soviet High Command and their means of pursuing them.

It is, of course, a fallacy to forecast the course of hostilities between the Soviet Union and the Atlantic Alliance in any one theatre of operations. Southern, Central, Northern or Oceanic, in isolaton from war in all of them, though it is a fallacy implied in a great deal of what is said and written about the problems of the various NATO Commands. If the Politburo and the Soviet General Staff were to decide upon an offensive against the Allied forces and territories in the Mediterranean, it would, no doubt, be part of a general strategic plan to envelop or encircle the main concentration of their opponents' military forces, political interests and industrial resources in Germany and Western Europe, while its main naval and air power, launched from the north, would aim at destroying their intercontinental life-line of reinforcement and supply. At the same time the offensive would have its local objectives, the fortunes of which would be determined by the actual strength of the air, naval and land forces in the area and the morale of the combatants.

On the Soviet side, it is probable that the two TVDs'[3] each with its political and military strategy, battle staffs and planned co-ordination of land, bomber and missile forces are involved in this Region, one for the Balkans, the other for the Near East/Central Asian area. The ground forces of the Soviet Union itself would consist of 27 or 28 motorised rifle and tank divisions drawn from the Odessa, North Caucasus and Transcaucasus Military Districts, probably with the 102 Guards Airborne Division deployed in the Odessa Military District and the 104 Guards Airborne Division deployed in the Transcaucasus. There would be co-ordination with the Black Sea Fleet which furnishes the 5th Escadra in the Mediterranean. In theory the total of the Southern Tier of Warsaw Pact forces could be built up to 54 divisions if all the three satellites' forces concerned joined in the act. But the ten Romanian divisions could not be counted upon as their government would probably try up to the last moment to remain neutral. The Bulgarians' ten divisions and recently augmented air force could be used, if compelled, against Turkey; but the speculation is that these two countries would serve mainly as rapid transit zones for the motorised Soviet divisions driving south and south-west. The four Soviet divisions stationed in Hungary would certainly come into play, and very likely some of the six Hungarian divisions for action in Yugoslavia.

Erickson, in his lecture notes on this subject[4] takes as his premise:

> that Soviet operations will open with a conventional phase of some duration, though this would not preclude a resort to nuclear weapons in a subsequent phase. The object of the conventional operations would be to advance with such speed and to such a depth that NATO's use of nuclear weapons would be virtually pointless.

In discussing the possible 'options' of the Soviet Command in the same notes he says:

> The Soviet command has no choice but to attempt to 'get' the U.S. Sixth Fleet and to neutralise U.S. Navy strike capabilities,

all for a variety of compelling reasons: pushing the strategic threat away from the southern regions of the U.S.S.R., forcing a way through the access points, securing the whole land approaches, cutting NATO lines of communication (and conceivably taking out NATO oil supplies by hitting the production points). ... Timing and time-tables can ony take on added significance — three days to take the Turkish Straits may fit in with Soviet time-tables and two airborne divisions could be used for key tactical purposes.

The initial duel between the US aircraft carriers and their escorts and the Soviet 5th *Escadra* would be a severe test of strength, with concentrated SSM attacks by Soviet missile cruisers and other vessels as well as attacks by the *Backfires* and other land-based bombers.

The defensive and counter-attacking capabilities of the US ships, however, are being constantly strengthened as, for instance, with anti-SSM systems which include the F.14 Tomcat, of which four squadrons are available to each of the two carrier task forces. The missile capacities of the Italian, Turkish and Greek navies are also not negligible. On the whole it is quite likely that the initial battle would not result in the Soviets' securing naval control of the Aegean, which would be a prior condition of success for their offensive as a whole.

Their operations on land would be concentrated, according to the same authority:

upon the rapid occupation of Thrace and the Turkish Straits in order to gain access to the Aegean; to the East, an attack on Eastern Turkey would be the first step to building a 'land bridge' to Syria and Iraq. The other 'land bridge' would start with the opening of operations to drive through sections of Yugoslavia, preceded by a push through Romania in the guise of Warsaw Pact co-operation, whatever the reluctance of the Romanians.

The defence of Northern Italy, which contains the greatest centre of industrial production in the whole of this region of Europe is, of course, conditioned by the fate of Yugoslavia. The collective leadership of that country would make every effort, sustained by such diplomatic aid as it could obtain from the United States,

Western Europe and its non-aligned friends, to uphold its independence. It is doubtful that it would call for, or receive, military assistance from the West before the outbreak of war and that, without it, it would fight in the face of a demand for the transit of Soviet forces.

> There are undoubtedly Soviet contingency plans to move into Yugoslavia. ... The Odessa M.D. has its own special head-quarters with its own staff of 'specialists', officers who have acquired first-hand knowledge of Yugoslavia — and are known through their 'tourist' guise to Yugoslavs — and the sub-command in this M.D., charged, not only with developing operational plans, but also forms of civilian administration in the event of Soviet action.[5]

If Slovenia fell into the Russians' hands the Italian Army and the Italian — American Air Force supporting it would have a hard task to hold the Gorizia Gap, the traditional gate of barbarian invasion. The defence of the north of Italy; the defence of northern Greece against invasion by the routes which two world wars have made only too familiar; of the narrow neck of Turkish Thrace, and of eastern Anatolia against invasion from the Caucasus, these are indicated as the four most probable battle-grounds. The first stage of hostilities, however, according to the known order of battle of the Soviets, would be their endeavour to 'take out' the nuclear capabilities of their opponents. This would involve an all-out attack on the 6th Fleet and the bombing of the cruise missiles in Italy and the US bases in Turkey and Greece.

Such is the picture which our experts trace of the probable onset of hostilities in the Southern Region, if the CPSU were to force them upon the Atlantic Alliance. The standard pretext of local revolution or liberation which has served to excuse military intervention in other parts of the world is not easy to find at present in this area; and the strength of the US Navy in this sea is itself an argument against the prospects of quick success. These are two reasons which diminish the probability of Russian aggression in this region in the immediate future. But no-one can foretell with any confidence the course of Communist imperialism after the end of the Brezhnev era. While there is time, every effort should, I am sure, by made by all the principal Western Allies to repair the manifest breaches in the defences of the Atlantic

Alliance, that is by strengthening the newly-restored co-operation between Greece and Turkey and restoring the consistency and credibility of the leadership of the United States.

16 Naval tasks within and beyond the Treaty Area

All the members of the Atlantic Alliance, with the single exception of Luxemburg, are

> maritime nations with substantial dependence on the sea lines of communication across the Atlantic. They include fourteen sea-going nations whose merchant fleets comprise 65 per cent of the world's total, whose share of all the tonnage being embarked and disembarked world-wide is also 65 per cent and who account for 40 per cent of the world's cargo in transit on the high seas. These same nations consume about two-thirds of the world's total oil production, about half of whose current supply is afloat at any given time.[1]

This is a good summary of the basic common interest of the Western Allies in the security of their sea communications, which it is the first and traditional task of their navies to protect. It is not a task confined to the North Atlantic; there is also, for the United States and Canada, the busy traffic of the Pacific, and we have noticed in an earlier chapter the intense seaborne trade of the Mediterranean. There are no seas in which the ships of the United States and their allies are not to be found in greater or lesser numbers, and we shall have to consider the vulnerability of their tankers and merchantmen in the Gulf, the Indian Ocean and the South Atlantic.

In assessing the functions of their navies in time of war, however, it is not difficult to see the particular importance of the sea area covered by the North Atlantic Treaty itself, for two reasons. It is in this area that the main sea lines of supply of energy, raw materials and food from Asia, Africa, Latin America and Australasia converge on their European and North American destinations; and it is here also that a constant stream of reinforcements and military materiel from West to East would have to be defended against naval and air attacks.

The Atlantic Alliance still has the edge over its potential opponents in the number of fighting ships, except for submarines,[2] though it is a little disingenuous to describe them as 'the most powerful Navy in the world'.[3] For it is not a single navy, as is that of the Soviet Union with its one permanent command structure, its single communications system and its single political direction. It is a collection of thirteen national fleets, one very large, three of medium size, nine relatively small, not all of whose ships come under the actual direction of an Allied Commander even in time of war. Despite these disadvantages, the standard of co-ordination and joint exercises of the United States, British, Canadian and West European ships allotted to SACLANT and CINCHAN (the Commanders-in-Chief of the Atlantic and the Channel Commands) is improving, though the diversity of communication systems remains a weakness. The standard of Allied co-ordination in the Mediterranean cannot be said to be brilliant, owing to the relative independence of the French in the west and the traditional animosity of the Greeks and Turks in the east.

The navy is a maid of all work. There are all manner of services which the navies may be called upon to discharge, from fishery protection to sea rescues, surveys and hydrographic research, showing the flag and attending to the needs of outlying dependencies. But we may group under four heads the basic tasks of the Atlantic Alliance fleets and supporting air forces, 1 protecting the trans-Atlantic lines of communication, 2 impeding the access of the Soviets to the Oceans, 3 defence of home waters, 4 protecting distant resources and lines of supply.

PROTECTION OF TRANS-ATLANTIC COMMUNICATIONS

It is hardly possible to foresee the role of trans-Atlantic shipping in a nuclear war. Indeed the issue might be so quickly determined by the exchange of intercontinental ballistic missiles, with the consequent devastation and dislocation of the belligerents that the regulation of sea transport became almost irrelevant. But that is not the kind of war for which the great variety of new surface ships, submarines and naval aircraft that Admiral of the Fleet Sergei Gorshkov has built up, seems to be mainly intended. Interception of an enemy's lines of communication is one of the principal objects of naval warfare which he has defined. It is consequently a war fought with conventional weapons, however sophisticated with which we are concerned in these notes. If such a war were prolonged for weeks or months, it is very probable that a shortage of escorts for trans-Atlantic convoys would soon be a serious problem. The reason for this is the advantage of the offensive in modern maritime warfare.

> It is important to appreciate that, unlike the situation on land, the defence of ocean sea routes require stronger forces than those of the attacker. For example, four or five enemy attack submarines deployed along a sea route would have to be countered by a considerable number of ships, aircraft and perhaps submarines if we were to be sure of tracking them down and eliminating them. Similarly, to provide adequate air defence around a force attacked by a handful of well-equipped strike aircraft may call for a large number of ships fitted with surface to air missile systems, plus carrier-borne fighters and early-warning aircraft.[4]

The US Navy, which is the largest in the world in surface combat vessels, is often regarded as the principal safeguard of trans-Atlantic communications. It is true that an escort force of about 250 ships, of which some 210 would be active warships was until three or four years ago provided for in the official American naval programmes, and it is estimated that 'the total 1987 level is likely to stand at 198 active ships'.[5] The primary mission of the escorts, however, including the modern ASW/AWW destroyers is not, in the view of the Pentagon, to protect convoys, but to protect the aircraft carriers.

> Indeed convoy operations are stated to require less capable escort forces because they involve protection of relatively slow moving ships in special formations against residual threats that have survived other barriers. Thus reserve warships, Coast Guard cutters, and allied warships have been included in force-sizing exercises for convoy protection operations.[6]

So it is in keeping with this doctrine, which certainly pre-dates the Backfire menace, that we find in the Congressional Issue Paper for the Fiscal Year 1981, that the United States relies on its allies to:

1. Contribute to barrier defences that restrict the Soviet Fleet's access to major sea lanes;
2. Provide escorts to protect convoys travelling the sea lanes;
3. Ensure the safe passage of convoys in restricted waters and entrances to major ports.

On the third point, it is agreed that the defence of convoys approaching Britain and the European coasts through the Eastern Atlantic falls to the Channel Command.

This is the main responsibility of the Royal Navy and the RAF, the Belgian, Dutch and German navies and air forces under a British Commander-in-Chief, with whatever co-operation the French can offer, after providing for their Mediterranean commitments. It is obvious, however, that the US Navy would have the major part to play in protecting convoys bringing reinforcements of troops, equipment and supplies for their own forces and their allies in Europe. The truth is that Congress has given too little attention of late to the navy's general requirements in the world war which an offensive of the Warsaw Pact against NATO in Europe would inevitably become, apart from its preoccupation with the nuclear ballistic missile submarines and the carrier battle groups. Protection both of east-west communications and of the flow of oil and other essential imports from the south could be a matter of life or death and clearly calls for the closest co-operation between the US, British, Canadian and West European fleets and maritime control aircraft, whatever the division of labour, under the overall direction of SACLANT.

Submarine attack, taking account of the experience of two World Wars and the great number of Soviet attack submarines,[7] is the most obvious threat to the Atlantic convoys. A great deal has been done to develop and improve anti-submarine warfare devices (ASW) by all the allied navies — as well as by the Soviets. Twelve of the allies co-operate in SACLANT's anti-submarine warfare centre at Spezia in Italy. Research is continuous. The United States have for some time been developing the bottom-mounted sensor surveillance system (SOSUS), from which a towed sensor array system has been evolved. A variety of ASW weapon 'platforms' (i.e. aircraft and vessels from which they can be discharged) are in service with all the thirteen Allied countries which possess navies. These include, besides the aircraft-carriers which might be available in the Atlantic[8] some 440 patrol aircraft and 300 helicopters belonging to states bordering the Atlantic. While most of the European NATO countries, because of the cost, concentrate their ASW efforts on coastal waters, there is reason to believe that the Allies' ocean-going ASW is efficient. Destroyers and fighters would have to form the bulk of the escorts. Excluding those required in the Mediterranean, the Channel Command, the Baltic and the Pacific, the Allies would seem to have some 240 escorts, mainly American, British and Canadian, available for the Atlantic patrols. I can well believe that SACLANT finds them insufficient.

But of more immediate danger than the submarine to the shipping of the western allies, as we have noted in the chapter dealing with the northern theatre of war, is the long-range Soviet bomber. Mr Duffy, in his speech on 19 June 1980 on the naval problem, which I have already quoted, said:

> It is significant that Soviet naval aviation received the *Backfires* before the Soviet Air Force. There are 40 to 50 naval *Backfires* in the Northern and Baltic fleets, all armed with PGM and anti-ship missiles. With refuelling their range could extend from the Kola to well south of the Azores. It is estimated that they are capable of sinking 20 to 40 ships a day, compared with the two, three or four per day sunk by the U-boats in the 2nd World War.

IMPEDING SOVIET ACCESS TO THE OCEANS

To protect convoys of merchantmen and transports against missiles launched by supersonic bombers is a task which has never confronted the defenders in maritime warfare before. It is evidently by attacking this new menace at source and intercepting it before it can reach the main shipping lanes that there is the best chance of thwarting the deadly danger. And this leads us to consider the second and even more important strategic task of the navies and maritime air forces of NATO, which is to block, so far as possible, the eruption of Russian power from its home bases into the Oceans of the world. This also is the job of the Supreme Allied Commander Atlantic and one which requires different and more varied implements than does the actual protection of shipping. But it confronts the Alliance also on a global scale. It has always been assumed that a maritime alliance would have the advantage over Russia, the great Euro-Asian land power, because its naval exits to the open sea could be blocked. That still applies to three of the four Soviet Fleets, the Baltic, the Black Sea and the Pacific, because the mining and blockading of the Baltic Approaches to the North Sea and the Turkish Straits would have a reasonable prospect of success (though we have seen in other chapters the difficulties involved) and both the southern and northern passages leading from the Sea of Japan to the Pacific could be made precarious for warships based at Vladivostok. In the case of the Northern Fleet, which is the most formidable, there is no such physical impediment to its access to the North Atlantic, except for the need to move between the southern limit of the Arctic Ice, in the Barents Sea and the northern tip of Norway. South and West of that there are only the interstices between Greenland, Iceland and Scotland (the G-I-UK gap) through which the Soviet submarines, bombers and surface ships would have to pass before reaching their hunting ground. The object of the NATO strategy is therefore to take full advantage of these narrows to establish a series of choke-points and barriers, so constraining its opponents to run the gauntlet and facilitating attacks by interceptors.

American planners envisage interceptor squadrons both at Keflavik in Iceland and in Britain, and there would also be a number of interceptor planes operating from aircraft-carriers in the Norwegian Sea and the North Atlantic. The F-14, whose Phoenix system enables it to fire at six targets simultaneously is the most powerful American interceptor aircraft. The nuclear-powered US submarine would play the most important part in the barriers designed to confine approaching enemy submarines and surface craft to the channels in which they could be more easily attacked, and long-range shore-based aircraft would be an essential element of the gauntlet system. A formidable aircraft for this purpose is the P.37 which, in addition to carrying up to eighty-seven Sonobuoys for detecting submarines and an armoury of ASW weapons 'also carries magnetic anomaly detective equipment to determine the exact position of submarines by means of changes they cause in the magnetic field above the water's surface'.[9] For purposes of convoy-escort the American P.3 and carrier-borne S.3 aircraft would co-operate with the British

Nimrod squadrons and the Canadian Maritime Control squadron, which are being updated. This is some indication of the extent of detailed Allied preparation for detecting and destroying as many as possible of both the bombers and the submarines emerging from the stronghold of the Soviet Northern Command to harass Atlantic shipping.

Much is being done to improve the Atlantic Allies' early warning system in this area, which is doubtfully adequate to cope with the capacities of the Soviet Naval Air Force. US and British airborne early warning systems compensate to some extent for the deficiencies of the land-based radar sites of NADGE (the NATO Air Defence Ground Environment network) in Norway, Denmark and Germany, such as the important North Cape Station in Finnmark, which are vulnerable to land and sea attack. (No land-based radar is usable in Iceland because the US — Icelandic Agreement confines US personnel to the low ground about Keflavik: hence AWACS is a necessity).

It is against this main strategy of canalising and confining as far as possible Soviet outbreaks from the Kola base and obstructing the exodus of the Baltic Fleet that the deployment of the Allied navies in the Atlantic — North Sea area has to be viewed. However effective the strategy may be, we can be sure that in Admiral Gorchkov's global planning there would be a number of Soviet submarines, cruisers and other commerce raiders and probably a couple of aircraft carriers in the open seas and outside confined waters at the outbreak of war. The allies would therefore have to be prepared to fight a variety of naval actions, quite apart from the defensive operations in the Atlantic which we have been considering. The recently acquired bases and supply ports in Africa, Southern Arabia, South-East Asia and the Caribbean would give the Soviet ships valuable means of continuous operation, but that does not compensate for freedom of movement to and from their permanent home ports and dockyards: it is this that, in any prolonged contest, the opposing navies would endeavour to deny them.

DEFENCE IN HOME WATERS

Quite different from the oceanic tasks of the allied navies and air forces is the actual defence of the approaches to their home ports, coasts and coastal shipping and, in the case of the North Sea allies, off-shore oil and gas wells. There are not many places on the Atlantic coasts that are likely targets for direct naval attack. But in the Mediterranean and Adriatic the Soviet Union's 5th Escadra might well do great damage to Italian, Greek and Anatolian harbours and installations and, of course, there is the whole of the Black Sea coast of Turkey to defend. In the Baltic the battle to prevent Warsaw Pact landings on the Schleswig-Holstein coast and the Danish islands would be likely to require all the Federal Republic's destroyers, frigates and fast-attack craft and land- and air-force co-operation, as well as the small Danish forces, with all the help that the Luftwaffe, RAF and Royal Navy could spare.

Airborne Soviet landings to capture the southern Norwegian airports and harbours in order to secure control of the Skaggerak must also be expected as well as similar onslaughts in the extreme north of the country. Apart, from being prepared to cope with such direct attacks, however, there is the problem of dealing with the naval mines which might well become the principal threat to ocean shipping approaching British and West European ports and to the coastal shipping and fishing fleets of all the European allies. Mine-detecting and sweeping are already minor tasks of every navy, but, in the event of a general war, this is likely to require quite a large force of specially built or adapted vessels, naval personnel and auxiliaries. Mr Keith Speed, the British Navy Minister, announcing a plan to add new counter-mine vessels to the Royal Navy said:[10]

> A fourth major threat to our ships and submarines in wartime would come from naval mines. The Soviet Union has large stocks of these weapons which can be laid from submarines, ships and aircraft, and the continental shelf around North-West Europe is particularly vulnerable.

PROTECTION OF DISTANT RESOURCES AND LINES OF SUPPLY

For the first time, I believe, since the formation of the North Atlantic Alliance, we find in the Annual Statement on the British Defence Estimates for 1980 a definite affirmation of a requirement, continually stressed by the military leaders of NATO and as continually ignored hitherto by their political masters, that 'in addition to our key NATO task, our defence policy should also be designed to help protect, wherever possible, our own and more general Western interests over a wider area, including those outside the NATO area'. After taking account of the opportunities seized by the Soviet Union and its allies to advance their own, and reduce Western influence in important areas, such as the Middle East, Southern Africa, the Caribbean and the Far East, and the increasing capability of the Soviet Union, aided by its Warsaw Pact and Cuban allies, to intervene in the third world, Mr Pym, the British Defence minister asked 'How should the West respond to the global threat to its interests?' The best answer was to try to remove the sources of regional instability; diplomacy, development and trade had a great contribution to make, and many forms of defence assistance can give support to friendly nations.

> Over and above this, the West must make it clear to the Soviet Union and its Allies that it is capable of protecting essential interests by military means should the need arise. That task cannot and should not be left to the United States alone. Of our European partners France has major defence commitments in Africa and elsewhere and retains permanent forces in the Indian[11] and Pacific Oceans. Vessels of the Federal German, Italian and Dutch navies undertake occasional deployment beyond the NATO area. Belgium provides training assistance to Zaire. All such activities help to protect Western interests world-wide. Against this background the Government believe that the Services should also be able to operate effectively outside the NATO area without diminishing our central commitment to the Alliance. . . . We hope that NATO as a whole will increasingly recognise the global nature of the Soviet challenge; and that the Alliance members, who are, like the United Kingdom, able and willing to counter the challenge, will consult before doing so and, where appropriate, act together. We shall give the strongest encouragement to such recognition and consultation within the Alliance.

This is an important declaration of policy, akin to the American notion of what the United States expects of its allies in defence of its sources of energy in the Middle East, but more balanced, in that it does not assume, as President Carter did in his reaction to the Iranian and Afghanistan crises, an automatic obligation of his allies to adopt measures of questionable value outside the scope of the Atlantic Treaty. The British appeal to their partners, who are willing to counter the Soviet challenge to consult and, when agreed, to act together, is realistic. It wisely leaves the weaker brethren to their Tropic of Cancer. It does not expect France to take part in a NATO exercise. It is the larger Allied countries, the United States, the United Kingdom, France, Canada and possibly Germany which are likely, in their own interests, to co-operate in opposing Soviet policies of expansion in other parts of the world.

What would they find it necessary to protect? Here we come directly to the question of whether we have in view preventive measures in times of peace, or whether we are thinking of war. Mr Pym's 'protecting essential interests by military means' is a euphemism for war: and, of course, though all sensible people hope that a war will not come, it is precisely to fight, and not lose a war against the Soviet Union 'should the need arise' that every provision of national and Allied defence is designed, whatever label of 'deterrence' it wears.

If we are concerned with the occasional deployment of naval ships in the Arabian Sea or the Caribbean or in African waters simply as symbols of what the Americans, or we, or the French might do if there were attacks on our shipping, or trade, or military intervention in the area — and that is really what the presence of an American or French aircraft carrier, or a British flotilla in the Indian Ocean or American aircraft on the Diego Garcia atoll really amounts to, no one can deny that it may help to restrain the Soviets from new adventures. That is worth while. It will not do even that, however, unless the CPSU believes that the powers concerned mean business and, if provoked, are prepared to fight.

Let us then consider the prospect realistically. In the first place it is futile to imagine that a war between the Soviet Union and its satellites and the principal Western powers could be localised; that oil wells in Saudi Arabia and the tankers which they fill could be defended by naval action in the Gulf, or cargoes of strategic minerals from Southern Africa defended in the South Atlantic, without hostilities occurring everywhere. With which states would the Western belligerents, beginning with their navies, be engaged? Not, surely, the Soviet Union alone, nor the Soviet

Union and its mainly land-based Warsaw Pact allies. Cuba is the main catspaw of the Russians in Africa, and Cuba, like Vietnam, Angola, Mozambique, Ethiopia and the People's Republic of Yemen, are all bound by mutual defence treaties to Russia. It is prudent to assume, therefore, that in the event of war they would all be more or less directly involved in denying to the Atlantic allies the oil, minerals and other supplies normally imported in large quantities from Arabia, Central and Southern Africa, as well as interfering with the important interests of the United States and the Europeans in the Caribbean. Port facilities and over-flying rights would be refused by these states and very likely by a number of other nominally unaligned states in Africa and Asia — India for one — unwilling to offend the Soviets. Considerable naval forces would be needed, depending upon how the naval duel in the Atlantic had fared in its early states; and all the ASW to which I have referred in the Atlantic context would be required, for instance, to cope with the nest of Soviet submarines for which fortified pens are being constructed at Aden and which would probably be the main source of danger to tankers in the north of the Indian Ocean. Control of the Straits of Hormuz would require sea, air and land operations on both shores, for which the co-operation of a greatly strengthened Oman would be needed.

The dependence of Britain, Western Europe and to a certain extent United States on strategic minerals is very great — 100 per cent of imports in the case of chrome, which comes from the South African Republic and Zimbabwe; and to get the cargoes safely home they would need continuous naval and air protection, particularly as they neared the 'Atlantic narrows' between Cape Verde and Cuba where the maximum effort at submarine interception must be anticipated. No doubt the Allies would not feel the withholding of mineral supplies in the early days of war, but, except for the United States which for some years has had a stockpiling policy (recently improved by the Strategic and Critical Materials Stock Piling Revision Act, 1979) it could become critical in a matter of weeks.

All minerals are strategic, some more than others. Chrome, manganese and varadium are essential ingredients of steel, and chrome of special alloys used in military aircraft and other armaments. Platinum is essential in the refining of oil; it is used in the production of glass and platinum group metals are used in electronic equipment. The proportion of these minerals that is put to strategic uses would increase very substantially in time of war.[12]

The sea transport of these mineral cargoes from South Africa is one question. Another is the safe shipment of copper and manganese ore from Zaire and Zambia, most of which used to come on the Benguela Railway to Lobito, still out of operation owing to civil war in Angola, but now dependent in ports in Zaire, Mozambique and Tanzania. It might well be necessary for the Western Allies to take offensive action in order to secure essential footholds for their naval operations around Africa. Brigadier Bidwell and his collaborators in their imaginative *World War 3* make no bones about the United States itself seizing and operating Simonstown, which seems a rather drastic way of obtaining an advantage which intelligent diplomacy could secure. But the dockyard and its neighbouring radio station would be of the utmost value to the Allies in protecting their shipping on the Cape Route. The Americans in any case would be obliged to neutralise Cuba, the main Soviet naval and air base in the Western Atlantic.

In short the tasks of the navies of the Western Powers in protecting their economic interests all over the world 'should the need arise' cannot be insulated from all manner of political implications. For instance, there would be the attempts of many non-aligned states in Asia and Africa, let alone the European neutrals to avoid siding with one belligerent or the other and the pressure of the belligerents to obtain facilities from them. Would Australia and New Zealand, in virtue of the ANZUS Treaty join in the fray? The attitude of Japan would be of crucial importance to the American naval position in the Pacific. At what stage would NATO as a whole become involved? These are but a few of the developments which are likely to attend the Western Powers 'protecting essential interests by military means' outside as well as within the Atlantic Treaty Area. It is right that they should be frankly faced. There is a better prospect of deterring the Communist Party of the Soviet Union from new ventures of revolutionary imperialism if the principal Western Powers show their readiness and ability to defend their rights in and around every ocean, than there is by hiding their heads in the sand.

Part Four

Some Defence Problems of the United Kingdom

17 Some aspects of the defence of the United Kingdom

RESERVES: AIR DEFENCE: CIVIL DEFENCE

In the third part of this book we have looked at what the Atlantic Alliance as a whole, and Britain as a member of it, would have to do in order to fight and defeat a general offensive of the Warsaw Pact if, despite every endeavour to deter it, it occurred. Next I should like to consider a few practical questions concerning the preparedness for such a crisis of the armed forces, administration and population in the United Kingdom. The three aspects of the question of which this chapter treats are the mobilisation of the Reserve Forces; Air Defence; and Civil Defence.

The Reserves

These consist of the Regular Army Reserve and the Territorial Army for the land forces, the Royal Navy and Royal Marine Reserve forces and the Royal Air Force Reserve. On paper their number is impressive. The total of those who could be called up, in view of their commitments, from the end of their service with the Colours to the age of 45, or 55 in the case of certain naval ratings and marines, together with those who have enlisted in the Territorial Army[1] comes to 207 500. But the number who could in fact be mobilised quickly enough to reinforce the 1st British Corps (BAOR) in Germany — the primary purpose of the auxiliary land forces — is far smaller than the total eventually available. The reason for this is that it is only the Independent (as against Sponsored) elements of the Territorial Army, who are trained and organised in units, mostly battalions, with their own centres and permanent staffs, who are ready to be integrated into the formations of the British Corps and go into action. Their actual strength is approximately 60 000.

The Regular Army Reserves, who would be called up individually and not in units, would be of great value up to, say, four years after leaving the army since they would have the necessary skill and experience to handle the weapons and equipment currently in use; after that they would most likely be posted, on recall, to home defence duties. The Reservists, other than officers, have an obligation to do two weeks' training a year, but in fact they have never been required to do any. The total number of the Army Reserves is given as 75 000; but in the new mobilisation plans announced by the Ministry of Defence in November 1979, which is intended to improve their readiness, it is 50 000 only who are to be issued in 1980 with uniform and equipment to be kept at home. This plan requires the Reservist to report annually to a local unit — instead of his, possibly, far distant regimental depot — where his fitness for a particular role will be assessed; and he may be required to do some refresher training. This is certainly less casual than the existing state of affairs, but it is an extraordinary contrast to the regular refresher courses for all ranks, from private to general, which are so important a feature of the Soviet Army Reserve.

> The two principal tasks of the Regular Army Reserves on mobilisation would be to make good shortfalls in the strength of the Territorial Army owing to under-recruitment and untrained recruits and to reinforce on an individual basis units of the BAOR which are below war establishment.[2]

I should imagine that, once fighting started, the replacement of casualties in Germany would absorb a great many of the available Reservists.

Several questions need to be answered. First, are the reinforcements which Britain could contribute to NATO in the event of war sufficient? I cannot believe that they are in view of the losses which the great weight of armour and air power of the Warsaw Pact could inflict on the Central Front in the first ten days. Voluntary enlistment is the only way of increasing this number. It is too late to revise the question of some form of national service, which, of course, obtains in all the other European NATO countries, though some form of military training and discipline could be salvation of tens of thousands of boys and men now condemned to the moral rot of unemployment. Vigorous recruiting to swell the strength of the Territorial Army should, I believe, be a government priority and be encouraged in every secondary school. The immediate aim should at least be to make up the 4000 Rhine Army men now tied down in Northern Ireland, for I am very sceptical, for the reasons given above, of the possibility of recalling them to Germany in time.

But the question which most worries the politician is the method and timing of mobilisation. In the German Federal Republic the Minister of Defence can call up 30 000 of the special Army Reserve without a decision of the Bundestag but no such half-way house is possible in this country. There is no possibility of calling up any element of the Army Reserves except by Royal Proclamation, now that the 'Ever Readies' have been abolished.

There are two reasons for the great political reluctance to proclaim mobilisation. One is the fear, grounded in history, that the mobilisation of one state or military alliance would provoke the mobilisation of its potential antagonists and, in the case of the Soviet Union, this might give the pretext for a pre-emptive strike. In fact, however, the group of Soviet forces in Germany, owing to its superior strength and ability to launch an offensive from a standing start, is far less dependent on reinforcement than is any of the Atlantic allies. The other reason is the danger of starting a panic in the civil population. On this point one can discern a certain amount of complacent self-deception in official quarters. For instance, in the Report of the Expenditure Committee of the House of Commons on Reserves and Reinforcements, to which I have already referred, we read:

> Our national military plans and procedures, as well as those for civil support of the Armed Forces, are closely co-ordinated with those of NATO. In a period of rising tension the implementation of these plans would be controlled by the Government of the day, with the object of effecting a smooth transition from peace to war of both the nation and the armed forces. Mobilisation and reinforcement would form part of this process.

What a hope! I cannot recall any historic case of 'smooth transition from peace to war' in this century; and I am sure that, though a 'surprise attack' by the Warsaw Pact, while technically possible, is unlikely, it is pretty certain that, however prolonged the preliminary rumblings, the attack, if and when it came, would be very quick and very devastating. There is no specific against panic other than telling the people the truth about the impending danger and taking practical and visible precautions well in advance.

This leads to the question of how long it would take to move our reinforcements into position. I have the best authority for estimating that the Territorial Army, which as we have seen is geared for movement in organised units, could be in position to reinforce that 1st British Corps on the Central Front in a minimum of ten and a maximum of fourteen days. This involves exact planning of transport by sea and air, which I believe has been well done. How soon other reserves could take up the tasks for which they are destined would depend upon whether or not hostilities broke out while the call-up was in progress. One can well imagine, for instance, that communications might be so disrupted by air raids as to make chaos of the postal service on which the raising of the Army Reserves is based. Subject to these disturbing thoughts, we could depend upon the Royal Naval Reserve, about 5500 strong, taking up its mine counter-measure duties in two or three days; and if the Anglo—Netherlands Marine Commando were rushed to the north of Norway—as planned—the small Royal Marine Reserve would be quick to reinforce them. Of the various categories of men and women who make up the 33 000 RAF Reserve it is likely that only a small number of trained specialists drawn from the RAF Volunteer Reserve would be recalled immediately. As for the main body of Army Reservists, how long would it take for the individual letters of recall, with travelling expense warrants, etc. to reach them if it depended upon the vagaries of the Royal Mail, for it is difficult to see how mobilisation by radio and television could be effected?

The Parliamentary Expenditure Committee was assured by the Post Office in May 1977 that 'the guarantee of 12 to 24 hour delivery time for recall notices still stood'. Most people in Great Britain, accustomed nowadays to wait for at least a week for letters to be delivered, will, I fear, be sceptical of this guarantee. The Ministry of Defence[3] states that the Reservist 'on call out will report to a local mobilization centre irrespective of cap badge; subsequent movement plans have also been stream-lined and more time will be saved'.

Air Defence of the United Kingdom

It is not necessary to be versed in the technicalities of modern military aircraft or electronic warfare to realise, as the shrinking numbers of the Royal Air Force made visible to anyone, that the air defence of the United Kingdom had, until the early 1970s, little more than a symbolic value. In 1972 there were, in this country, only five squadrons of Lightning fighters, and one of Phantoms for maritime defence. There were no surface-to-air missiles, our Bloodhound squadrons having been moved to Germany, no air-borne early warning, and the Linesman command and control organisation, which was co-ordinated with a system of civil air control, had proved to be hopelessly inadequate. The British indeed played their part in the 2nd Tactical Air Force of NATO in Germany and it was there that the worth-while fighter squadrons of the RAF were located. The reason for the absence of any systematic air defence was the same as that which allowed civil defence, as we shall see, to fade away like the grin of the Cheshire cat. It was not that the possibility of a Soviet attack was ignored: it was the mistaken belief, upon which British defence policy had been based since the fatal Defence White Paper of 1957, that the threat of massive nuclear retaliation was the only, and sufficient means to deter it.

For this NATO's conventional forces provided the trip-wire; the American strategic missiles were, in theory, to be brought into action by any attack upon members of the Atlantic Alliance; and Britain's contribution to this nuclear deterrent was its four missile-launching Polaris submarines and its ageing Vulcan bombers. This served as a sufficient excuse for successive British Governments to cut defence costs and to neglect the defence of the United Kingdom against conventional attack by sea, land or air. We have seen in earlier chapters how and why this doctrine of nuclear retaliation has fallen into disrepute and how NATO since 1977, and with it the British government, have adopted the doctrine of flexible response, which means readiness to meet attack at any level. Since the rapid expansion of the Soviet Union's conventional land, sea and air forces is the most striking evidence of its present strategy, the restoration of an effective system of air defence of Britain and its surrounding waters, is now being energetically undertaken. But it takes years to bring a new, sophisticated military aircraft into service.

The United Kingdom Air Defence Region (UKADR) is a sub-command of the European Command of NATO. The duty of its Commander is to defend targets within the region and to contribute to the NATO battle for air supremacy by destroying as many enemy aircraft as possible. Since it was decided to phase out the Royal Navy's aircraft carriers, he is also responsible for maritime defence within flight-refuelled range of the RAF's shore-based fighter aircraft. The strategic importance of the UKADR to NATO, and its attraction as a target for Soviet attacks, are enhanced by the fact that Britain is an essential staging-point for the US Air Force engaged in Europe and a platform for the proposed cruise missiles.

On 17 April 1980 an important air exercise was organised by NATO, called 'Elder Forest 80' to test the defences of the UK Air Defence Region. The defenders were all the fighters (including Hawk jet trainers) which the RAF could muster in Britain plus United States F-15 Eagles from West Germany and F-5s based in Britain, representing the American planes which would be moving through Britain in the event of war. Though the RAF had 90 fighters theoretically available, only 65 were in fact able to take to the air. The defenders numbers about 100 aircraft in all. The attackers, representing the Warsaw Pact, were a joint force of 240 planes made up from the air forces of United States, Belgium, Canada, France, Germany, the Netherlands and Denmark. Airfields, ports, radar stations, military bases, rail and road networks and bridges were their targets. Though a final verdict on this exercise has not, I believe, been issued, the assessment is that many of the attacking planes got through and that the defenders suffered proportionately higher casualties in aircraft and air crews than did the RAF in the Battle of Britain in 1940.

In reality the outcome of such a mass attack, if made by the latest Soviet supersonic bombers, the Sukhoi SV-19 Fencer and the Backfire in particular, would be devastating, and this gives us the measure of what must be attempted as soon as possible to defeat that threat. For example, an abundance of surface-to-air missiles would be an important contribution to the country's protection. SAMs would have put a different complexion on the 'Elder Forest' exercise, but there were said[4] to be only two squadrons of Rapier land-based defence launchers in the country.[5] SAMs are particularly needed to protect both American and British airfields, and it seems that (a financial dispute between the US Army and Air Force having been composed) the Americans will pay for sufficient Rapier SAMs to be made by British contractors to defend the American fields and will man them.

This is only one of several measures now being taken by the British government to improve air defence. The most important weapon development is that of the Air Defence Version of the Tornado of which 165 should be delivered to the RAF by the end of 1983. A qualified authority has written about this remarkable plane:

> The defensive capabilities of the *Phantoms* and their AWG 10 and AWG 12 weapon systems will eventually be outflanked and overtaken by the technological progress of the Warsaw Pact ECM equipment and techniques in the 1980s. The *Tornado ADV*, on the other hand, is confidently expected to have the capability to counter the *Backfire* and *Fencer* and their ECM support for as long as they remain the backbone of the Warsaw Pact's conventional air threat.[6]

This is encouraging, and we are told that 'Assuming a delivery rate of four aircraft a month, all 385 Tornados on order for the RAF (both versions) will have been delivered by the end of 1987.'[7]

Among other improvements in the armoury of the RAF is the replacement by 1981–2 of the aging *Shackleton* early warning aircraft by the *Nimrod AEW 2* whose system is fully interoperable with the NATO and American early warning systems. Older types of radar and communications are being replaced, and the improved United Kingdom Air Defence Ground Environment with its data-handling system will be able to obtain instantaneous target information from its own improved radars, NADGE, French and naval data systems and defence satellites. There is certainly an atmosphere of urgency and progress about the RAF nowadays which is a welcome contrast to the doldrums of yesteryear. What is needed now is to make the public conscious of the very real danger from the Soviet Union's formidable attack aircraft to this country which, in the sphere of air-power, has become so vital a link between the United States and Europe, and what is being done to meet the danger.

Civil Defence

To take every precaution which is practicable to protect the lives of the civil population in wartime is a logical corollary of the accepted obligation to defend the country against both conventional and nuclear attack. Yet in Britain, in marked contrast to the official policies and popular attitudes of our continental neighbours — not to speak of the massive protective shelters and evacuation measures of the Soviet Union — there is an extraordinary unwillingness to organise home defence. The reason for this is a psychological one: people just do not want to think about war and its impact upon their normal pursuits of material wellbeing. We have been for thirty-five years in a state of peace which a great part of our population imagines can be continued indefinitely by a process of wishful thinking. And nothing is more disagreeable to the politicians who seek the votes of this uninformed mass than a national programme of protection against air attacks, nuclear blast and radiation, chemical warfare, fire and destruction; for this implies that war is liable to become a reality.

It was in this spirit that in the mid-1960s a Labour Government, after reducing national expenditure on defence — a process which their Conservative successors continued — proceeded in 1968 to put Home Defence, which had been revived twenty years before, on a 'care and maintenance basis'. The Civil Defence Corps and the Auxiliary Fire Service were both disbanded. It was an odd, but typically insular position for the British Labour Party to take; for it is in fact the mainly Socialist countries of northern Europe with which it has the closest affiliations — Norway, Denmark, Sweden and the Netherlands in particular — which have developed the most thorough systems of civil defence. Norway gives detailed instruction on the subject in every telephone directory, including a map of directions for the evacuation of Oslo.

Mr Callaghan justified the running down of the Civil Defence mechanism because the government believed that any future international crisis would be preceded by a long enough period of escalating tensions to allow civil-defence operations to be organised and implemented. In fact the official policy assumes that this process would begin two or three months ahead of the expected attack. This is a very questionable belief. It is one that is very common to people of Mr Callaghan's generation, who remember the year of grace which elapsed between the first scare of war at the time of the Munich crisis and Hitler's invasion of Poland which actually began the Second World War. But there is really no ground for believing that this course of events will be repeated. Another reason for the prolonged unwillingness of the British to contemplate an aerial attack on these islands and all its disagreeable consequences is faith in their 'nuclear deterrent'. These are popular inhibitions and illusions which must be dissipated by the reasoned campaign which I believe to be urgently needed. It must show that a sensible system of home defence is a necessary contribution to the greater military efficiency of the Atlantic Alliance.

A good deal of attention has been given to this question in the last year by Members of Parliament, Civil Servants and the 'Quality Press' in this country. We have, for instance, a very well thought out plan[8] by two Conservative Members, Robin Hodgson and Robert Banks, who is Rapporteur of the Assembly of the Western European Union on Nuclear Biological and Chemical Protection. They insist, first, on reactivating the existing official skeleton of Civil Defence. Of this one part has survived intact though it is little known. It is the United Kingdom Warning and Monitoring organisation administered by the RAF for the Home Office and manned by the Royal Observer Corps, 10 000 strong; its purpose is to provide early warnings of attack and subsequent warnings of radio-active fall out. Its network of 873 undergound monitoring posts covers the whole country. The other part of the machine is in dire disrepair. Its essential feature is the division of the country into 13 regions, sub-divided into 24 sub-regions, each of which would be the effective unit of government in the event of nuclear war. Each is supposed to have a secure underground headquarters, but in fact few of these exist. Under the sub-region would come the metropolitan county, or county administrative unit, whose chief executive is responsible for civil defence.

This responsibility is in most cases devolved to a County Emergency Planning Officer. These gentlemen exist, and in a few counties, Wiltshire in particular, have aroused keen co-operation, but the majority, it is reported, have for months and years had nothing to do, though some occasionally attend courses at the Home Defence College at Easingwold, which takes its task seriously. According to the book of words, three or four weeks ahead of an expected enemy attack the sub-region would come to life, its headquarters would be continuously manned (By whom?) and the public might be encouraged to lay in stocks of food and clothing. Only three days before the anticipated descent of bombs and missiles would the government mount a massive publicity campaign in the Press and on radio and television, advice on making primitive 'do it yourself' shelters would be shown on cartoon films (which have been made) and a booklet 'Protect and Survive' would be delivered by the postmen to every home. It is hard to conceive a more inept and pusillanimous way of facing what might be a deadly peril to the whole population.

The main points of the Hodgson — Banks proposals are that the Civil Defence Act of 1948 be amended, giving the central government power to compel local authorities to ensure that the minimum standards of home defence planning are met; that there should be a special Home Defence Committee in the Home Office under a Minister; that an inspector of Home Defence be appointed, whose annual report would come before parliament; that public information on home defence be improved and should in particular give practical advice (as in other countries) about strengthening the structure of houses so as to provide shelter; and that the Warning and Monitoring Organisation's communications equipment should be brought up to date so as to lessen its vulnerability to attack. Other recommendations are that the network of underground sub-regional and county headquarters be quickly completed; that every local authority should carry out a shelter survey; that a network of ward and parish emergency centres be organised and that the local authorities must prepare for the enrolment and good use of volunteers, including representatives of local industry, and arrange for the co-operation of the Reserve Forces of the armed services in their area.

All these proposals seem sensible, and I agree with the authors that the present 'no shelter, no evacuation' policy should be revised. I am sure most people would welcome a plan for the maximum number of home shelters, with tax and rates concessions to encourage it, and for the use of all existing underground tunnels, tubes and storage space in towns for collective protection. The strain on public order accompanying planned evacuation, especially from the neighbourhood of airfields and other particularly vulnerable military targets, would be far less than the panic which might erupt in an atmosphere of *sauve-qui-peut*. A most important aspect of the steadying of public opinion, which I have not seen mentioned in any publication on the subject, is control of the media of information in the tense atmosphere of anticipated or actual attack. The familiar freedom of comment and debate by radio commentators would be intolerable in such circumstances. It would be necessary for the government to assume absolute responsibility for all radio and television broadcasts.

It is important that, in preparation for this great trial, which may, but we hope will not, fall on the country, the authorities should take the citizens into their confidence and not treat them as children from whom disagreeable truths are concealed until the last moment. Appalling as is the prospect of a thermo-nuclear attack, there could be many survivors, with the maximum use of shelters, such as the Norwegian and Swiss have planned, and the co-operation of public spirited people. But for the reasons already suggested in these pages, attacks with conventional explosives would seem to be the more probable danger, if the Soviet Union, despite all deterrent efforts of the West, were to launch a war. Obviously, the enemy might resort to nuclear weapons, depending upon the course of conventional hostilities. But it is against the kind of aerial attacks which were experienced in the Second World War, that the defenders would most likely have to react; and this involves, apart from the technique of anti-aircraft defence, the best available shelters, judicious evacuations, fire-fighting and all the rescue and ambulance operations which are inseparable from conventional warfare.

Notes

NOTES TO CHAPTER 2: SOME ILLUSIONS TO BE DISSIPATED

1. Cf. the extract from Henry Kissinger's speech at San Francisco, 3 September 1976.
2. Joseph Comblin, *Théologie de la Révolution* (Paris: Editions Universitaries, 1970).
3. In a paper on the meaning of *détente* at the Annual Conference of Atlantic Organizations, Hamburg 1976.
4. Two days of Congressional Hearings on this subject in April 1979 produced a densely printed volume of 500 pages.

NOTES TO CHAPTER 3: THE STRATEGIC SITUATION TRANS-FORMED

1. Laurence Martin, 'A Dangerous Imbalance', BBC Radio 3 broadcast, printed in the *Listener*, 15 November 1979.
2. Which, it is fair to remember, the United States, had already proposed in the United Nations, should be abolished by an agreement which the USSR refused.
3. Henry Kissinger's speech in Brussels, September 1979.
4. **Defence Expenditure**
   Mr Churchill asked the Secretary of State for Defence what was defence expenditure in each of the past 20 years expressed at constant prices; and what is the estimated expenditure to 1984-85.

   Mr Pym: The information requested is set out below. All figures are at 1979 survey prices. However, for the years 1960-61 to 1963-64 actual expenditure figures are not available at constant prices, and estimates figures have been given. The figures for the years 1980-81 to 1983-84 were published in Cmnd. 7826-I in April 1980. No planned expenditure figures are yet available for 1984-85.'

DEFENCE EXPENDITURE AT 1979 SURVEY PRICES (*£ million*)

	Estimates*	Actual expenditure*	Plans
1960-61	8,593	—	—
1961-62	8,523	—	—

(*continued*)

	Estimates*	*Actual expenditure**	Plans
1962-63	8,685	—	—
1963-64	8,895	—	—
1964-65	—	8,775	—
1965-66	—	8,901	—
1966-67	—	8,954	—
1967-68	—	8,926	—
1968-69	—	8,485	—
1969-70	—	7,995	—
1970-71	—	7,962	—
1971-72	—	8,016	—
1972-73	—	7,942	—
1973-74	—	7,832	—
1974-75	—	7,518	—
1975-76	—	7,864	—
1976-77	—	7,719	—
1977-78	—	7,540	—
1978-79	—	7,486	—
1979-80	—	7,709†	—
1980-81	—	—	8,001
1981-82	—	—	8,243
1982-83	—	—	8,490
1983-84	—	—	8,745

* Because of changes in the defence budget definition, the revalued figures in prior years are only an approximate indication of comparative expenditure.

† Provisional figure, consistent with Cmnd. 7841.

Source: Her Majesty's Stationery Office, *Written Answers*, 31 July 1980.

5. The three per cent increase in real terms was achieved in 1978 — 9. In the years 1979 — 80, 1980 — 1, the increase was below three per cent as a consequence of the economic difficulties facing the Conservative Government.

6. In Chapter 1 of this book.

NOTES TO CHAPTER 5: STRATEGY OF THE CPSU

1. Lord Brimelow, *The Meaning of Détente*, Conference of Atlantic Organizations (Hamburg, 1976).
2. Walter Ulbridat. Published in *Deutschland*, 18 December 1960, quoted by Lord Brimelow, op. cit.
3. 'The Concept of Power and Security in Soviet History', Adelphi Paper. No. 151.
4. See p. 47 this work.
5. See p. 83.

6. General Hackett *et al.*, *The Third World War* (London: Sphere Books, 1979).
7. Vice-Admiral B.B. Schofield, in *World Survey*, no. 62 (1974).
8. Leon Gouré, William G. Hyland and Colin S. Gray, *The Emerging Strategic Environment*. Special report for the Institute for Foreign Affairs Analysis Inc.

NOTES TO CHAPTER 6: SOME INTERNAL CHARACTERISTICS AND PROBLEMS

1. Sir Fitzroy Maclean, *Sunday Telegraph Magazine*, 23 March 1980.
2. Jerry F. Hough and Merle Fainsod, *How the Soviet Union is Governed* (Cambridge, Mass.: Harvard University Press, 1979).
3. Hough and Fainsod, op. cit. 'The table is based on the detailed occupational categories in the census.'
4. Hough and Fainsod, op. cit.
5. Sir Fitzroy Maclean, *Sunday Telegraph Magazine*, 23 March 1980.
6. Soviet Economy in a New Perspective (Joint Economic Committee, Congress of the USA, 1976).
7. *The Three Banks Review*, March 1980.
8. From *The Right to Believe*, no. 1 (Keston College, 1980).

NOTES TO CHAPTER 7: THE MILITARY ORGANISATION OF THE SOVIET UNION

1. John Erickson, *Soviet Military Power* (RUSI, 1971), gave an estimate of twenty per cent.
2. Herbert Goldhamer, *The Soviet Soldier* (London: Leo Cooper, 1976).
3. James Turnbull, *The Soviet View of War as an Instrument of Policy*, in Erickson, *Regional Development in the U.S.S.R.* (NATO, 1979).
4. Erickson, op. cit.
5. Erickson, op. cit.
6. David Holloway Adelphi Paper, No. 152, p. 15.
7. David Holloway, Adelphi Paper, No. 152, pp. 25 — 6.

NOTES TO CHAPTER 8: SOVIET ARMAMENTS: PRESENT STRENGTH

1. Lord Hill Norton, *No Soft Options* (London: Hurst & Co., 1979).
2. Divisions, brigades and similar formations aggregated on the basis of three brigades to a division.
3. Sergei Gorshkov, *The Sea Power of the State* (Oxford: Pergamon, 1978) quoted by Lord Hill Norton in his *No Soft Options*.
4. That is to say, aircraft carriers. cruisers, destroyers and frigates.
5. Col. E. Asa Bates Jr., *RUSI Journal* (June 1978).
6. *Outer Space. Battlefield of the Future*, SIPRI (1978).

NOTES TO CHAPTER 9: PROSPECTS OF THE PROJECTION OF SOVIET
POWER

1. Two particularly valuable guides are Peter Vigor's *The Soviet View of War, Peace and Neutrality* (London: Routledge & Kegan Paul, 1975) and John Erickson and E.J. Feuchtwanger (eds). *Soviet Military Power and Performance* (London: Macmillan, 1979).
2. In Erickson and Feuchtwanger, op. cit.
3. Ibid., p. 199.
4. Ibid., p. 207.

NOTES TO CHAPTER 10: PROPAGANDA AS AN INSTRUMENT OF
POLICY

1. Hough and Fainsod, *How the Soviet Union is Governed* (Cambridge, Mass.: Harvard University Press, 1979).
2. 1938 Communist Congress Report. Quoted in Ian Greig, *The Assault on the West* (London: Foreign Affairs Publishing Co., 1968).
3. See Generals da Luz Cunha, Kaúlza de Ariaga, Bethencourt Rodriguez and Silvério Marques, *A Vitória Traída* (Braga and Lisbon: Intervencão LDA, 1978).

NOTES TO CHAPTER 11: THE PROBLEM OF UNITY AMID DIVERSITY

1. See p. 79.
2. Brigadier Shelford Bidwell *et al.*, *World War 3* (London: Hamlyn, 1978).
3. General Hackett *et al.*, *Third World War* (London: Sidgwick & Jackson, 1978).

NOTES TO CHAPTER 12: NUCLEAR ARMS AND POLICES

1. Declaration of the Second Vatican Council (1963 — 5), *Gaudium et Spes, 80*.
2. Lenin, address to the Third All-Russian Congress of Communist Youth.
3. 'Honeste fastidium', Leo XIII would have called it.
4. IISS, *Strategic Balance*, 1979 — 80.
5. *Strategic Options for the Early Eighties* (New York; National Strategy Information Centre Inc., 1979).

NOTES TO CHAPTER 13: THE NORTHERN THEATRE OF OPERATIONS

1. *Soviet Military Digest*, Defence Studies (University of Edinburgh).
2. *The U.S. Sea Control Mission*, Background Papers (Congress of the United States, 1977).

NOTES TO CHAPTER 14: THE CENTRAL FRONT

1. IISS, *The Military Balance in 1979—80*.
2. E.g. George H. Quester, in *Encounter*, 27 August 1978.
3. *NATOs 15 Nations* (April/May 1979).
4. I am indebted to Normal L. Dodd's account of 'The British Army of the Rhine', in *Defence*, November 1979, for detailed information in this section.
5. If the British Corps is still there.
6. German — American Round Table on MBFR 1980.
7. Cf. my book *Warning and Response* (London: Leo Cooper, 1978).

NOTES TO CHAPTER 15: THE SOUTHERN THEATRE OF OPERATIONS

1. Admiral Shear's speech at change-of-command ceremony of the 6th Fleet at Gaeta, 16 July 1979.
2. Admiral Means Johnson Jun.'s lecture at RUSI, 12 February 1975.
3. See chapter 7 in this book.
4. *Soviet Options and the Southern Flank.*, Defence Studies (University of Edinburgh, November 1978).
5. Ibid.

NOTES TO CHAPTER 16: NAVAL TASKS WITHIN AND BEYOND THE TREATY

1. A.E.P. Duffy, MP, former Under-Secretary of State for Defence for the Royal Navy, speech in the House of Commons, 19 June 1980.
2. The totals were given for purposes of comparison with the Soviet Navy in Chapter 8 in this book.
3. *NATO Review*, December 1979.
4. Vice-Admiral Sir James Jungius, *NATO Review* (December 1979).
5. US Sea Control Mission, Congressional Budget Office, Washington D.C.
6. Ibid. Quotation from Annual Defence Dept Report 1975.
7. The total number of the Soviets' nuclear and diesel-powered submarines is approximately 340.
8. Of the twelve US carriers now in service, two are normally in the Pacific, two in the Mediterranean, and two in overhaul. One, the 91 000-ton *Nimitz*, has been in the Arabian Sea since the Soviet occupation of Afghanistan.
9. The US Sea Control Mission.
10. House of Commons, 19 June 1980.
11. Base facilities for a squadron have been retained at Djibouti and the high mountains of Reunion, a Department of France, are of considerable value for radar.
12. Christopher Coker, South Africa's strategic importance: a reassessment *RUSI Journal* (December 1979).

NOTES TO CHAPTER 17: SOME ASPECTS OF THE DEFENCE OF THE UNITED KINGDOM

1. Called the Territorial and Army Volunteer Reserve until November 1979.
2. Sixth Report of the Expenditure Committee of the House of Commons 1977.
3. November 1979.
4. John Fullerton, *Now*, May 1980.
5. The US Cruise missiles which are to be stationed at bases in Berkshire and Cambridge in 1983 will be defended by RAF-operated Rapier SAM missiles.
6. Air Commodore P.S. Collins, Director of Forward Policy (RAF), Ministry of Defence.
7. Michael J. Getting, *Defence*, October 1978.
8. *Britain's Home Defence Gamble*, Conservative Political Centre.

Index